Comebacks

Andrea Redmond
Patricia Crisafulli

Comebacks

(Powerful Lessons from **Leaders**
Who Endured Setbacks and
Recaptured **Success** on Their Terms)

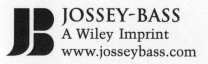
JOSSEY-BASS
A Wiley Imprint
www.josseybass.com

Published by Jossey-Bass
A Wiley Imprint
989 Market Street, San Francisco, CA 94103-1741—www.josseybass.com

Readers should be aware that Internet Web sites offered as citations and/or sources for further information may have changed or disappeared between the time this was written and when it is read.

Limit of Liability/Disclaimer of Warranty: While the publisher and author have used their best efforts in preparing this book, they make no representations or warranties with respect to the accuracy or completeness of the contents of this book and specifically disclaim any implied warranties of merchantability or fitness for a particular purpose. No warranty may be created or extended by sales representatives or written sales materials. The advice and strategies contained herein may not be suitable for your situation. You should consult with a professional where appropriate. Neither the publisher nor author shall be liable for any loss of profit or any other commercial damages, including but not limited to special, incidental, consequential, or other damages.

Jossey-Bass books and products are available through most bookstores. To contact Jossey-Bass directly call our Customer Care Department within the U.S. at 800-956-7739, outside the U.S. at 317-572-3986, or fax 317-572-4002.

Jossey-Bass also publishes its books in a variety of electronic formats. Some content that appears in print may not be available in electronic books.

Library of Congress Cataloging-in-Publication Data

Redmond, Andrea.
  Comebacks : powerful lessons from leaders who endured setbacks and recaptured success on their terms / Andrea Redmond, Patricia Crisafulli.
      p. cm.
  Includes bibliographical references and index.
  ISBN 978-0-470-58375-3 (cloth)
  1. Chief executive officers—Case studies.   2. Leaders—Case studies.   3. Success in business—Case studies.   I. Crisafulli, Patricia.   II. Title.
  HD38.2.R435 2010
  658.4'2—dc22

                                                                      2010004757

Printed in the United States of America

FIRST EDITION

HB Printing   10 9 8 7 6 5 4 3 2 1

Contents

With love and gratitude:

For Bill and Duke
—A. R.

For Joe and Pat
—P. C.

Introduction:
When the Rug Gets Pulled

A t some point in life, the rug gets pulled from under us. We get
fired. A long-awaited promotion does not materialize. A
business fails. Our health suffers. A relationship—in business or
in our personal lives—ends. No one is immune. Regardless of job
title or level of achievement, an upset of some type is inevitable.

For most people, a professional setback such as getting fired
is a private matter. Dealing with the aftermath, from the emotional
upheaval of being rejected to the career uncertainty, happens
behind closed doors. For high-profile leaders, however, circumstances are much different. In addition to dealing with
the intensely private issues that go along with a career upset,
the events surrounding their setbacks are often played out very
publicly. Suddenly every detail becomes fodder for media com-
mentary and analysis. Previous successes and failures are chronicled in news stories (often with inaccuracies), and unflattering
pictures are splashed everywhere. Private upset becomes public
embarrassment.

This fact became clear to Andrea seven years ago, when she sat
down with Jim Cantalupo, a long-time McDonald's Corporation

executive and then CEO of the company, to discuss leadership traits for a book project in which she was involved. In the two-hour conversation that followed, Jim and Andrea established an instant rapport and their discussion deepened. As Jim reflected on his life and career, he shared what it had been like for him a few years prior when he lost out on the CEO role at McDonald's and left the company feeling defeated and dejected. He had been within a millimeter of becoming CEO, only to lose the job he wanted—and his family and friends heard the news on television and read about it in the newspaper. Later, Jim was asked to return to the company and was brought in as CEO.

A short time after this conversation, Jim Cantalupo died suddenly. The story he shared stayed with Andrea for years. She began reaching out to CEOs who were terminated, offering a word of encouragement or to be a sounding board. When Andrea met Tricia, who at the time was writing *The House of Dimon*, a leadership profile of JPMorgan Chase CEO Jamie Dimon and the ultimate comeback story, they realized that there was a deep story to tell about what happens when leaders go through setbacks and their process to recapture success on their terms.

In *Comebacks*, we share the stories of ten high-profile leaders who experienced a serious upset in one form or another—such as being fired or asked to resign, quite possibly due to circumstances that were at least partially beyond their control. Often the termination happened suddenly and unexpectedly. Many said they did not see it coming, describing their termination in words such as being "blindsided" and "sucker-punched."

Being fired as the leader of a large firm often triggers a media blitz that most of us will never face. And the obvious should be stated: A CEO who is fired does not have the same financial worries (if any at all) as the rest of us who lose a job. However, we all know what it's like to feel embarrassed and vulnerable, and to be caught up in self-doubt and second-guessing. Based on these commonalities, there may be much to learn from the experiences of these

CEOs and other leaders who managed to maintain a sense of self in the midst of great turmoil: how they picked themselves up, redefined their priorities, took accountability and responsibility where appropriate, and created and explored new possibilities and directions.

As we discovered, sometimes those lessons came in the form of twenty-twenty hindsight, as people saw and acknowledged what they could or should have been done differently. Other times, the lessons involved strategies for coping, such as resilience, self-knowledge, and relying on family, friends, and other close supporters. Having endured a setback, they learned or affirmed that their identities are not the same as their job titles; that a balanced life must constitute more than just a job. The lessons were as varied as the individuals themselves.

Equally interesting were the leaders' second acts. Each person's choices were unique and fitting to his or her circumstances, personality, preferences, and stage in life. Regardless of how one bounced back, success for each person was defined on his or her terms. Whether a person decided to pursue another leadership position or went off in an entirely different direction, essential to taking the next step were evaluation of one's goals and priorities and an appreciation of what matters most. Only then could they clearly weigh the opportunities in front of them. Collectively, the stories in *Comebacks* show that there is no one way or right way to endure a setback. The way forward is a course that people must chart for themselves.

Patricia Dunn's strategy for facing felony charges related to the corporate spying scandal at Hewlett-Packard while she battled cancer was to make a "cosmic distinction between those I knew and didn't know. . . . " To endure difficult days of being vilified in the press, she relied on the support of family, friends, current and former colleagues, and others who reached out to her. "If the world had gone silent," she said, "I would have been devastated."

For Christopher Galvin, being asked to step down as CEO of Motorola, the company founded by his grandfather, just as a turnaround he had put in place was coming to fruition, was deeply painful. To endure the setback he relied upon inner resources of resilience that allowed him to "gut it out." As he observed, "Nobody can talk you out of what you are feeling. People say all kinds of nice things, but that doesn't take away the pain."

Following a setback, most of the leaders we interviewed advocated taking a break, physically and mentally, in order to avoid making a rash career decision. Jamie Dimon, now CEO of JPMorgan Chase, explained that after being fired as president of Citigroup in November 1998 he engaged in "a thought process" to figure out his next step. "What did I want to do? I didn't want to fill up my calendar before I decided what I wanted. I wanted to decide," he said.

Others bridged the transition differently. David Neeleman responded to the upset of leaving JetBlue Airways, which he had founded, by focusing on what he could do next. Even as he continued to process the emotional upheaval of leaving behind the company that was his "baby," Neeleman launched his next venture. As a servant leader dedicated to helping others, Neeleman found it was better to "find something else to focus on. . . . Think about people other than yourself."

Focusing on others also helped Dale Dawson decide what to do in the second half of his life when, after selling his business, he suddenly lost the passion that had always spurred him ahead. His response was to employ his business skills as an executive and investment banker in a completely new arena—a place in the world where there is deep need and great potential. His story stands as a dramatic example of being willing to rethink one's life and career and to redefine success. "Are you being led where you need to go?" Dawson observed. "If not, don't be afraid to walk away."

In the midst of a career disappointment, a common experience is to return to one's roots. After stepping down as CEO of Ford

Motor Company, Jac Nasser took several months off to return to Australia where he had been raised and where his ninety-eight-year-old father still lives. He also became grounded in the many lessons his father had taught him by word and example over the years. Nasser credited his father for having an "unwavering level of confidence and a belief that things will work out in the long term if you work at them."

Harry Kraemer, after resigning from Baxter International, relied upon his lifelong practice of self-reflection, which he adopted in high school and which is the cornerstone of his leadership today. Through self-reflection, Kraemer was able to look at his life honestly and with new perspective as he weighed his choices of what to do next. "You have to take some time to really stop and think through what you are all about," Kraemer explained.

David Pottruck, who left as CEO of Charles Schwab & Company where he had worked for twenty years, has also engaged in an honest and candid self-assessment of his strengths and accomplishments— as well as his shortcomings and failures. A former college athlete who distinguished himself in football and wrestling, Pottruck had endured disappointments before in his life, but always managed to move on to new successes. As he observed, "There are always setbacks. Success in life demands the ability to bounce back."

Each of the executives who navigated through career storms was challenged to reassess his or her goals, beliefs, character, and sense of self. For Herbert "Pug" Winokur, being a long-time outside director on the board of Enron Corp. put him in the crosshairs of scrutiny when the firm imploded in the midst of allegations of fraud. Through years of testimony, from Congress to creditor panels, Winokur was sustained by the knowledge that he and other outside board members had acted in good faith based upon the information that was presented to them by company management. Therefore, he was able to separate what was happening around him from what was happening to him. "You have to accept that it's not about you at all," Winokur observed.

In the midst of a setback, it is tempting to sink into feelings of self-doubt and or even defeat, believing that every previous accomplishment has been negated. Not true. A career is not a single episode. An array of experiences, both positive and negative, comprises all that a person has accomplished. Durk Jager, former CEO of Procter & Gamble, worked for the company for thirty years, including several years in top leadership positions. Although he had to step down as CEO, Jager's assessment of his career is summed up in a powerful statement: "I have done my best."

The leaders profiled in *Comebacks* generously contributed their stories, describing details of their lives and careers, which led ultimately to reaching a pinnacle of achievement. They also recounted not only what happened when the rug was pulled from under them, but also how they felt at the time, and what they needed to do in order to move forward again. Their stories are related in *Comebacks* without judgment and are told primarily from the viewpoint of the corporate leader. Our intention is to give you a view through that leader's eyes, to understand what it was like to be on top of one's game one minute and then sidelined the next. For some of those profiled, this is the first time that they have spoken at such length and depth about their experiences from setback to comeback. Without the candor of those we profiled, *Comebacks* never would have been possible. We salute them for sharing their stories and their wisdom, and we applaud their willingness to demonstrate courage and vulnerability in order to share their lessons with the rest of us.

Comebacks

I don't think the American dream is to start a company and sell it. Sometimes you end up selling your dream. There are things that money can't buy.

—DAVID NEELEMAN, FOUNDER AND FORMER CEO OF JETBLUE AIRWAYS CORP., FOUNDER OF AZUL LINHAS AÉREAS BRASILEIRAS

Chapter One

DAVID NEELEMAN
WHEN IT'S TIME TO MOVE ON

Every time David Neeleman has faced a career upset or disappointment, he has quickly responded by pursuing the next opportunity. His phoenix-like determination to rise from the proverbial ashes has led Neeleman, now fifty, to establish no less than three airlines thus far. His entrepreneurial drive has been fueled by a creative vision to establish organizations that are as good as, or even better than, their competitors, and in the process to help other people.

"From the time I sold my first company when I was thirty-three, it has always been about creating new things and helping people reach their potential. Money is a way to keep score at times I suppose, but it doesn't bring happiness. Money is the means, but it's not the be-all and end-all," Neeleman said.

Neeleman's fondest creation was JetBlue Airways Corp., which from its first flight in 2000 quickly captured both news headlines and customer loyalty for its superior service and commitment to do whatever possible not to cancel a flight. An ice storm in February 2007, however, delivered a black eye to JetBlue's nearly unblemished record, an unfortunate event that Neeleman labeled "the worst operational week in JetBlue's seven-year history."[1]

Although he may not have been personally at fault for the nightmare of flight cancellations that extended for days, as chairman and CEO, Neeleman took responsibility for the crisis. His public apologies were followed by an even greater commitment to

1

customer service to restore JetBlue's reputation. For Neeleman, however, another storm was brewing, as discussions ensued around who would be best to oversee the day-to-day operations of the airline, which had been his brainchild and fondest creation. Only three months later, in May 2007, Neeleman was asked to step down as CEO and a year later relinquished his chairman's title as well.

Neeleman may have been temporarily without an airline, but he was far from grounded. His latest venture was already taking shape in his mind, an opportunity in Brazil, which is his second home and a market in which he sees untapped potential. This new venture would allow Neeleman once again to build a business embracing the philosophy of servant leadership: putting the needs of others first to inspire them to give of themselves and reach a higher level of achievement.

Devoting himself to this new business in Brazil and focusing on the needs of his employees is how Neeleman copes with his departure from JetBlue, a loss over which he had little control. The man who has been called "a serial entrepreneur" relies on his philosophy of servant leadership and generates momentum through new ventures to carry him forward into the future, even though the pain of past setbacks remains.

Growing Up in Brazil

A seventh generation Mormon, David Neeleman and his family hail from Utah, but his personal roots are in Brazil. His father, Gary, had been a Mormon missionary to Brazil as a young man, spending two-and-a-half years in the southern part of the country and in Sao Paulo. Even after Gary returned to Utah and got married, Brazil was close to his heart and he longed to go back. He became a foreign correspondent for United Press International (UPI) and soon became the Sao Paulo bureau chief during his seven years there as a correspondent. (Several years later he became UPI's vice president over Latin America and the Caribbean.) The second oldest of seven children, David Neeleman was born in Brazil and grew up speaking English and Portuguese. When Neeleman was five, his father moved the family back home.

Back in Utah, Neeleman faced a difficult transition to elementary school. Born in October, he was younger than many of his classmates, a situation that became compounded when he was moved ahead a grade because he had already attended kindergarten in Brazil. Later he was diagnosed with attention deficit disorder (ADD), which further explained why school was so challenging for him.

Neeleman benefited from another type of education: working at his grandfather's grocery store from about the age of nine until he was nineteen. Watching his grandfather interact with people who came into his store, Neeleman learned quite a bit about customer service. Then came his first real taste of success, which molded him as a leader. At the age of nineteen, Neeleman was sent to Brazil as a missionary, thanks to his dual citizenship and the fact that his father had previously served the church there. During his two-year mission, Neeleman rose through the ranks of district leadership and served as district president for the last seven months of his assignment. "For the first time in my life, I succeeded at something," he reflected.

His time in Brazil, spent mostly in the northern part of the country, also exposed Neeleman to a different side of life among people who were largely poor and very humble. The contrast between haves and have-nots created an indelible impression. On one hand were the wealthy who enjoyed a sense of entitlement; on the other were the poor who had next to nothing and yet were often happier and more willing to share what little they had. His experience in Brazil would later affect his leadership in the airline business in many powerful ways.

But as a young man returning to Utah from Brazil, airlines were not on his horizon. Soon, however, he would have his first experience in the travel industry, which would quickly immerse him and, despite an early failure, would never get out of his blood.

Entering the Travel Business

After returning home from his mission to Brazil, Neeleman married his girlfriend, Vicki, and entered the University of Utah. While still a student, he started a travel business in the early 1980s, renting timeshares in Hawaii. "Because of the recession at the time, companies couldn't sell time shares, so I said, 'I'll rent them for you.' That's how I got started," Neeleman recalled.

When an airline agreed to sell him tickets wholesale, Neeleman was able to offer airfare and accommodation packages to his customers. By the time his company reached twenty employees and $8 million in sales, Neeleman had to drop out of college as a junior to run the operation full-time. Then the airline that had sold him tickets went bankrupt, and Neeleman had to make restitution to his customers. It was a considerable financial loss that nearly wiped him out. "I was done with the travel business," Neeleman remembered thinking at the time.

Married with two children, Neeleman had no choice but to join his in-law's window-covering business and went back to work for his grandfather's grocery store to make ends meet. It didn't take long for the next opportunity to come along—and, once again, it was in the travel business. In 1984, June Morris, founder of corporate travel agency Morris Travel, whom Neeleman described as "a very wise lady," invited the then twenty-four-year-old Neeleman to join her company and develop a leisure travel business. Neeleman accepted her offer and set up a charter air service which later became Morris Air, the first airline he helped to establish and of which he became a part owner. With Morris Air, Neeleman realized his destiny as an entrepreneur in one of the most difficult, cost-inefficient, and otherwise challenging industries. "This was my first airline—my first hit," he recalled proudly.

Based in Salt Lake City, Morris Air was among several low-cost airlines that challenged larger carriers on shorter, regional routes. In 1992, while at Morris Air, Neeleman developed a ticketless technology that was a breakthrough innovation in the industry. (Although Southwest Airlines is often credited for having invented ticketless travel, Neeleman says it all started with Morris Air.)

The success of Morris Air attracted the attention of Southwest Airlines, which in December 1993 agreed to buy the smaller airline in a stock swap worth about $129 million. Neeleman, then president of Morris Air, told the *New York Times* that a buyout by Southwest had not been a stated goal, but "was definitely something we had in the back of our mind."[2]

Being acquired by Southwest was a victory for Morris Air, enabling it not only to become part of a larger airline, but also to join forces with a company that was revolutionizing air travel with affordable fares and an expanding system of routes. "Southwest was a beacon that was out there," Neeleman observed in a speech he gave at Stanford University in 2003.[3]

The Southwest deal gave thirty-three-year-old Neeleman some $25 million from the sale of Morris Air and a new boss and mentor: Southwest CEO Herb Kelleher. "When Herb came to town we hit it off," Neeleman recalled. Both dyed-in-the-wool entrepreneurs with vision and charismatic personalities, Neeleman and Kelleher shared a deep passion for the business and a competitive spirit.

In our interview, Neeleman spoke with admiration for Kelleher, particularly the way he treated employees. "He could just sit and talk to someone. He didn't care who you were; he just liked people," he said. Neeleman was also influenced by Kelleher's ability to focus "more on the people instead of the profits." He recalled a comment Kelleher delivered at an analyst conference: "When I take care of them, they'll take care of the customers." Neeleman would go on to adopt this same attitude in the airlines he later founded.

After Morris Air was purchased, the plan was for it to be merged slowly into Southwest over two or three years, during which time the Morris Air planes were to be repainted and most employees would be hired by Southwest. The pace of that integration, however, was too slow for Neeleman who had grown Morris Air at a rapid pace. Although he loved Southwest and greatly admired Kelleher, Neeleman was told in 1994—a year after the merger—that he would have to leave. "I saw them running my company [Morris Air] as they were integrating it. I was trying to get them to be more progressive. Herb said to me, 'It's not working out. It's too disruptive for a big organization,'" he recalled.

It was a devastating blow for Neeleman who said he would have returned every penny of the $25 million he made on the deal with Southwest "to take my company back." That disappointment led to an important revelation regarding his ultimate motivation as an entrepreneur: It wasn't about the money. "I don't think the American dream is to start a company and sell it," he reflected. "Sometimes you end up selling your dream. There are things that money can't buy."

Even before his departure was official, Neeleman was already weighing possibilities for his next venture. What he settled upon was helping to run a Canadian discount airline, based in Calgary, called WestJet. With a five-year U.S. non-compete agreement after he left Southwest, Neeleman decided Canada was "the closest place to Utah that was out of the country." In early 1996, Neeleman became an investor and a board member of WestJet.

During this time, Neeleman also developed Open Skies, a reservation system that catered in particular to small and medium airlines, allowing them to issue electronic tickets. In 1998, he sold Open Skies to Hewlett-Packard, which, in turn, sold it in 2000 to a unit of consulting firm Accenture. Open Skies reflected Neeleman's belief that technology can create efficiency in airline travel. However, technology alone would not be the solution to better air service. As Neeleman believes, "There is a human aspect of our business. We are in the service business. We call it . . . high tech, high touch. You need to be able to do both."[4]

After WestJet and Open Skies, Neeleman had a strong desire to establish an airline that would be like no other. In 1999, as his five-year non-compete with Southwest was coming to an end, Neeleman looked around the U.S. market for what he could do next. His target: the Northeast, where airfares were particularly high. Going to New York on several occasions to speak with potential investors, Neeleman surveyed John F. Kennedy Airport, which he saw as wide open in terms of terminals and runway capacity. "So I decided to do it again," he said simply.

Starting his new airline, his second, Neeleman decided to learn from the mistakes of others, particularly when it came to poor customer service and the hassle of flying. He sought the advice of his longtime legal advisor Tom Kelly and financier Michael Lazarus of Weston Presidio as he explored the ways a new airline could use customer service as a competitive advantage. A case study by Harvard Business School summarized the brainstorming around Neeleman's new venture: "What if building a people-centric corporate culture could not only increase pride and creativity, but also avoid a unionized workforce that every major airline had, including Southwest? What if you could build a discount airline that had an entirely new fleet of planes? What if you could create an almost entirely paperless airline, with ticketless flying as the only option?"[5]

Neeleman answered all those questions with JetBlue. To fund it, he raised $130 million mostly from the original investors in Morris Air, with one notable newcomer: billionaire investor George Soros and his Quantum Fund, who at one point would own about a third of the company. Other investors included Chase Capital and Weston Presidio, which backed what Neeleman called a "Southwest-Plus" business plan. With investors onboard, Neeleman made JetBlue the best-funded startup in airline history.[6]

In July 1999, JetBlue was unveiled as "New York's new low-fare, hometown airline," promising affordable airfares that would be, on average, 65 percent less than current fares on some routes. Called the first "mega start-up" airline, JetBlue's initial plans were for a fleet of up to 82 new Airbus A-320 aircraft. JetBlue promised wider seats, more legroom, and more overhead storage space than other airlines in its class. Another plus was twenty-four channels of live in-flight television for a first-class experience in every row of the aircraft. "I was looking for something we could offer for entertainment. I still remember finding this company that could put live television in the seat back. When I saw it, I knew that was it. We were the first ones to offer it," Neeleman recalled, sounding very much like an entrepreneur who enjoys breaking ground and doing things, both large and small, before others do.

There were many firsts for JetBlue, which embodied Neeleman's vision of offering something different—or as he called it "a new shade of blue"—in air travel. These differentiators were more than just window dressing and amenities; they reflected a commitment to establishing a culture that was vastly different and that would translate into satisfaction and success.

"The vision for JetBlue came from everything I learned at Morris Air and WestJet, all of my experiences rolled into one, with a goal of becoming better than all of them. A lot of things I took from Southwest, such as how they treated people and how efficient they were," Neeleman said. His goal was not just to mimic but to significantly improve upon what he had experienced first-hand at other airlines. "My goal was to be a new and improved version of Southwest."

Although JetBlue would be a major accomplishment for Neeleman, there would later be deep disappointment in store for him as well. Before that happened, however, it would be one incredible ride.

At the Controls of JetBlue

Reflecting on his entrepreneurial drive, Neeleman explained it as the desire to figure out how to do something "better, more efficiently and at lower cost." At JetBlue, he first attracted an all-star team of industry veterans, including Dave Barger from Continental Airlines, who became chief operating officer; Tom Kelly as general counsel; John Owen from Southwest as chief financial officer; and Ann Rhoades, the senior human resources person at Southwest who had helped fire him, as head of human resources. Others came from Virgin Atlantic and the U.S. Department of Transportation. The team embraced Neeleman's core values of putting employees (whom Neeleman called "crewmembers") first as they worked to deliver the lowest-cost and highest-quality service.

JetBlue's first flights took off in 2000. By August of that year, which was only its sixth full month of operation, the airline posted a profit and boasted top-ranking on-time performance. "With JetBlue, we're proving that a start-up airline can be successful, popular and profitable," Neeleman said at the time.[7]

Looking back, Neeleman attributes JetBlue's success to having all the right ingredients: "We had the best product, the lowest cost, and the best service. Usually there is a trade-off, but we had all three, and that was the lynchpin."

During the economic downturn of 2001 and even after the tragic events of September 11—which took a brutal toll on the entire airline industry—JetBlue was able to grow. "While we initially reduced our flight schedule in the days following the attacks, we're currently operating the same number of flights today as we were on September 10," Neeleman stated at the time. "With an additional 18 daily flights planned, we will operate a total of 102 flights by the end of the year. Our growth plan remains intact and we are proud to say that we have not laid off a single employee, nor have we cancelled or deferred a single aircraft delivery."

The airline was profitable in the third quarter of 2001, a time when "most of our industry is reporting unprecedented losses," Neeleman added. He called the results a "great tribute to the dedication and hard work of the entire JetBlue team." He also credited the "resilience of our low fare, low cost business model."[8] For Neeleman, being able to announce positive news in the midst of an industry beleaguered with losses must have been immensely gratifying, an affirmation that his vision of offering higher service at a lower fare was possible—and profitable.

JetBlue was clearly flying high, and so was its hard-working CEO, who earned positive press and numerous accolades. A May 2003 feature in *Time* magazine described how Neeleman "obsesses over keeping employees happy," which also allowed it to stay union-free, which observers saw as critical for a low-cost carrier. JetBlue's turnaround times averaged 35 minutes, on par with Southwest, the industry leader. Innovative flight patterns and routes allowed it to avoid congestion and maintain its on-time record. Above and beyond these qualities, *Time* noted, "the best thing JetBlue may have going for it is Neeleman."[9]

Neeleman's Servant Leadership

With JetBlue, David Neeleman not only established an airline, he also created a culture that was truly different; where employees and customers alike would feel valued.

"This is something I say in talks that I give: Think of five successful companies that you love doing business with. Most people can't think of five," Neeleman said. His vision for JetBlue was to become one of those admired companies. Beyond his entrepreneurial drive and operational insight, Neeleman brought to JetBlue the lessons he learned back when he was a missionary to Brazil, where the divide between rich and poor never ceased to affect him. At JetBlue he sought to close distinctions among the ranks, including between top executives and the company's other crewmembers. "I was in the field at least once a week: serving snacks, loading bags, talking to pilots," Neeleman recalled. "I was totally comfortable doing that."

What Neeleman learned in Brazil about winning the loyalty, respect, and trust of others he applied at JetBlue to employees and customers. This is the essence of servant leadership, a phrase that was coined by Robert K. Greenleaf, founder of The Greenleaf Center for Servant Leadership. Greenleaf once observed, in an essay written in 1970, "The servant-leader is servant first. . . . It begins with the natural feeling that one wants to serve, to serve *first*. Then conscious choice brings one to aspire to lead."[10]

James C. Hunter, principal of J.D. Hunter Associates, a leadership training and development firm, explained the difference between management, which he described as "what we do," and leadership, which is "who we are," our character—the person we are when nobody is looking. "Leadership is our personal ability to influence and inspire people to action," he added.

The "servant" part depends on how the leader establishes authority and influence with others. "Building authority with people comes from serving and sacrificing for them," Hunter explained. "Being a servant, however, is not about being a slave. It's not about doing what people want; it's about doing what they need. What employees want and need may be two different things. In business, it's about identifying and meeting the needs of employees, such as respect, appreciation, and encouragement, and also setting standards and holding people accountable."

Based on his thirty years working with leaders in business, including many entrepreneurs, Hunter sees servant leadership as a key to success. Rather than being ego-driven, servant leaders strive to succeed out of a genuine desire to create opportunities and inspire others to achieve their potential. "People who are servant leaders are humble, authentic, and real. It's not about them. What keeps the servant leader awake at night is not, 'When am I going to get the corner office?' or 'what are my perks [perquisites]?' but 'do my people have everything they need to win?'" Hunter added.

At JetBlue, Neeleman's servant leadership promoted an egalitarian spirit. Distinctions based on rank or salary level were wiped out at the airline, such as no reserved parking for certain high-level employees and the same desks and chairs for the CEO as for others in the offices. Its planes, too, had only one class, and the most legroom was found in the back of the aircraft. No corporate plane for Neeleman either; when he had to fly, he sat in the jump seat with the crew. Neeleman's leadership extended to his treatment of the people onboard his planes, whom he refused to call "passengers." Instead, Neeleman referred to them as "customers," which conveyed the importance of selling a service that people want, rather than simply transporting them from place to place.

Neeleman's brand of leadership required a big commitment in terms of hours, many of which he spent in the air talking to customers and employees and gathering feedback and ideas that could make the airline even better. A 2004 *Inc.* magazine feature, which included Neeleman among "America's 25 Most Fascinating Entrepreneurs," noted that, two days before his interview, he "had been up at 4 A.M. to fly roundtrips from New York to Fort Lauderdale and then San Diego. He estimate[d] that he talked to 500 customers in the two days. . . . "[11]

Neeleman's habit of picking up trash after a flight landed or making notes as he met customers were not the only things that made him different among other CEOs. In his book, *The Mormon Way of Doing Business: How Eight Western Boys Reached the Top of Corporate America*, journalist Jeff Benedict called Neeleman's compensation package, which was also reflective of his servant leadership philosophy, an anomaly. "His annual salary is only $200,000 per year, plus an average of between $70,000 and $90,000 per year in bonuses. His donates his entire salary to a fund for his employees. Financially independent from the success of his previous business ventures, Neeleman is able to operate this way," Benedict wrote.[12]

Neeleman's adherence to servant leadership principles won him praise and respect—and it also produced results. In recognition of his innovation and achievement, Neeleman received the Tony

Jannus Award in 2005, given by the Tony Jannus Distinguished Aviation Society, which recognizes accomplishments in commercial aviation.

Everything Neeleman strived to do at JetBlue reflected the entrepreneurial advice he still gives to others today, from students to business leaders. "If you want to do something, make it the best," he said. "Make it the best model you can, and take care of your customers."

The sad irony, however, is that a colossal failure in customer service, the thing that JetBlue prided itself on above everything else, would become a major embarrassment and ultimately would contribute to the unraveling of Neeleman's career at the airline he founded.

An Ice Storm to Remember

It started with a cold rain on Valentine's Day, February 14, 2007, with no accumulating ice forecasted. Since it was the start of President's Day weekend with a busy travel schedule, JetBlue made the decision to allow multiple flights at Kennedy airport to depart their gates. But when the rain unexpectedly turned to ice, the planes were unable to take off. They were also unable to return to their gates since other planes had since occupied their slots at the gates. As a result, the customers whom JetBlue had vowed to treat better than anyone else were stranded on the tarmac for hours.

Although other airlines were hit by the ice storm, those carriers responded by cancelling more flights earlier. JetBlue, however, had apparently counted on the weather improving, which would enable it to keep flying, without disruptions to its customers— or its revenues. "On the contrary," the *New York Times* reported, "JetBlue's woes dragged on day after day. On Saturday night (February 17, 2007), for instance, the airline said that 23 percent of flights it had canceled on Saturday and Sunday would be canceled Monday."[13]

For JetBlue, which had been flying so high on accolades over its customer service, the incident was a nightmare. As the Harvard study noted, the day-to-day operations had been delegated to the chief operating officer, Dave Barger, who was in Florida when the storm hit and stayed there for several days. "Operating without his longtime COO at his side, Neeleman became all too aware of how ill-equipped JetBlue was to handle a crisis of this magnitude."[14]

Talking about the ice storm today, Neeleman expressed frustration and dismay over the logjam in JetBlue's operations, which resulted in the airline having to cancel flights for the next several days until crews and planes were finally in place to resume a normal schedule. In short, JetBlue had become completely overwhelmed, from reservation agents who couldn't handle the flood of calls from angry, displaced, and delayed customers to an inability to "reset" the airline quickly enough.

As horrific as the problems were, what was most notable about the February 2007 ice storm was Neeleman's immediate and public response. Suddenly he was everywhere, interviewed by the media and appearing on television to explain what happened and to offer apologies to customers. In a television interview with NBC's Matt Lauer, Neeleman acknowledged the weaknesses that the incident exposed in the JetBlue system, which resulted in flight cancellations extending for several days. He also pledged that the problems in reservations and crew assignments that had been exposed were already being addressed. "Accountability rests with the CEO, I think, even though I wasn't responsible for that particular part of the operation. That's why I spent three days and sleepless nights. I know exactly what failed and what can be fixed. And it will be fixed and is being fixed," Neeleman told Lauer.

Asked by Lauer if someone in JetBlue management would be fired over the incident, Neeleman firmly answered no.[15] What he did not know at the time, however, was that he would be the one who ultimately would have to step down.

Neeleman's public campaign to win back customers did not end with explanations and apologies. He also unveiled a "customer bill of rights" stipulating such things as notification of delays and cancellations and offering vouchers in the event of delays due to "controllable irregularities."[16] The customer bill of rights was unprecedented in the industry and remains unique today.

Although Neeleman won points with the public and praise from crisis communications experts, JetBlue's board disagreed with his decision to apologize for the crisis. Today, all Neeleman would say about the events that unfolded following his apologies is that the JetBlue board began to question whether he should take "more of a strategic role" while Barger ran the day-to-day operations. Neeleman opposed the plan, but in the end stepped aside at the board's request.

In May 10, 2007, JetBlue announced the appointment of Barger as CEO, while Neeleman would serve as nonexecutive chairman of the board. In a statement, Neeleman called the executive change a "natural evolution of our leadership structure."[17] Looking back on that time, however, Neeleman acknowledged, "I was tortured" by the board's decision, which was completely unexpected, especially since six months before he had received high marks from the board on his evaluation as CEO.

"It was horrible—really shocking. I felt like I was sucker-punched," Neeleman said. It seemed incomprehensible to him that he was being asked to step down from the helm of the airline that was his "baby," which he had brought from concept to success. To Neeleman, JetBlue was more than a business; it was an emotional investment of himself, his energy, and his best ideas.

Although being removed as JetBlue's CEO was personally devastating, Neeleman eventually used the experience as a lesson to share with others. "This is what I tell people who have to fire someone. I say if the person is going to be surprised, give them another chance." For him, however, there was no second chance.

Neeleman spent a year as the nonexecutive chairman of the board of JetBlue, and then in May 2008 he relinquished that position as well, thus ending his association with the company. He summed up his feelings in a "Farewell and Thank You" e-mail message. In the e-mail, which was addressed to "fellow crewmembers and friends," Neeleman admitted that this was a note "I never thought I would be writing."

Neeleman's words were emotionally powerful as he expressed his "considerable sadness" over the decision not to stand for reelection as chairman and acknowledged, "It has been difficult for me to be removed from the day to day management of a company that has been my life's passion for the past ten years." He also expressed his pride for JetBlue's accomplishments and gratitude for his colleagues. "We created one of the true (and rare) success stories in aviation history by challenging ourselves to do better in everything we do. I'm proud of you for your hard work, your loyalty to JetBlue—and most importantly, your commitment to each other."

Typical for Neeleman, as he was saying his final good-bye to JetBlue, he also announced the plans for his next venture: his third airline, Azul. As he noted in the farewell note, " . . . I have decided to dedicate the next phase of my professional life to building a world class airline in Brazil. . . . Brazilian culture, language, and spirit are in my blood and I've always wanted to return to the country of my birth and make a positive difference. I now have the unique opportunity to build an airline in Brazil with the same values, social responsibility, and crewmember culture that served as JetBlue's key foundational ingredients."

With that, Neeleman ended one venture with a note of regret, and moved on with hope to the next.

Working Through It

Although the transition after JetBlue has been difficult, Neeleman is working through it—literally. Being busy with Azul "has helped me not to dwell on it," he said. JetBlue, however, is not yet behind him. Neeleman's lingering emotional ties to the airline were evident when he described being invited to the dedication of a new JetBlue terminal at Kennedy Airport in October 2008. Since he had left the company six months previously, Neeleman was reluctant to go but was persuaded. "When I walked into the place about 3,000 people all stood up and started to cheer. It was spontaneous," he said.

What has helped him move on, however, is his ability to accept reality: His time with JetBlue came to an end. Now it is time to find something else to which he can dedicate his time, energy, and ideas. "You have to find something else to focus on—charity work or church or a civic organization," he said. "Think about people other than yourself. No one is going to care for your self-pity after all. You might as well start doing things for other people."

Neeleman's commitment to do for others, which reflects his servant leadership, has helped him move beyond disappointment to a new chance for success with Azul. It is a lesson he has learned several times before: when his first travel business failed, when he was fired from Southwest, and more recently when he had to leave JetBlue. As Neeleman observed in his farewell message from JetBlue, "We all have and must face difficulties and challenges in our lives. I have always believed that it is not what happens to you in life but rather how you respond to it that matters."

For Neeleman, the response has surely not been to sit idle or to spend too much time wondering what to do next. Although other executives we interviewed for this book advocate taking time off, particularly after a career upset, in order to process what has occurred and to decide what the next move should be, Neeleman takes at different tactic: He gets busy right away, although he acknowledged, "I'm not over it still."

Taking Off in Brazil

With his latest venture, Neeleman has gone back to his roots in Brazil, where he sees opportunity as well as a place to serve others.

An August 2009 feature in the *Economist* spoke of the size of the opportunity that Neeleman could potentially tap: a swelling middle class in Brazil, with about 97 million people who are "rich enough to contemplate" traveling by air. The magazine further assessed, "Making air travel more accessible in a country the size of the continental United States, where infrastructure is rickety and many families have been scattered by internal migration, is a noble aim—and potentially a lucrative one."[18]

Another positive factor is the plan to improve aviation infrastructure in Brazil before the country hosts the World Cup in 2014. Brazil will also host the 2016 Summer Olympics in Rio de Janeiro.

The Azul plan for the Brazilian market sounds very similar to what Neeleman accomplished at JetBlue: low fares and low costs on regional routes. Not only should this rack up profits for the airline, but it will also improve the quality of life for many people, as Neeleman sees it. Instead of taking a long and grueling bus ride, they will be able to fly Azul for about the same price.

Just as with JetBlue, profits are not his primary focus at Azul, which Neeleman is running along with a team that includes seven or eight people who came from JetBlue. That distinction belongs to the employees for whom Neeleman's approach is a welcome surprise. "We created Azul with the same values we had at JetBlue," Neeleman said. "The culture in Brazil is not necessarily a culture of servant leadership. Employees are often treated more like servants." Azul's approach of viewing employees as the most important part of the business is a "stark difference," he added. As a result, Azul has "virtually no turnover" among its 1,500 employees. Neeleman believes that these employees who feel appreciated will pass along that good will to customers, who in turn will have a positive experience.

Whereas Azul's operations benefit from Neeleman's successes at JetBlue, the organizational structure of the new operation is the direct result of his still-painful departure from his previous airline. "With Azul, I retained all the voting shares, not because I want to dictate, but so that I would not get sucker-punched again today," he said. "Today, I can't be fired."

At the same time, Neeleman is committed to keeping the Azul board of directors continuously updated on whatever is happening at the airline. These days, he must be telling a growth story for Azul, which launched in December 2008. From its hub at Campinas, outside Sao Paulo, Azul serves thirteen destinations in Brazil. By the end of its first year of operation, Azul flew its two millionth passenger, and became Brazil's third largest carrier. With an initial fleet of twelve 106- or 118-seat aircraft made by Brazil's Embraer, Azul has a total seventy-five planes on order, of which it will probably get another seven to twelve delivered in 2010.[19] "And," Neeleman noted proudly in late 2009, "we're close to profitability."

For Neeleman, Azul is another chance to create a legacy. In his book, *Firing Back: How Great Leaders Rebound After Career Disasters*, co-written with Andrew Ward, Jeffrey Sonnenfeld, who is Associate Dean for Executive Programs at Yale University's School of Management, described the need for leaders who suddenly find themselves out of a job to redefine what he called a "heroic mission." This may involve "a sense of accomplishment in creating a legacy" or "effecting change in society through building and leading an organization."[20]

By defining their mission and purpose, leaders create a strong foundation for the next opportunity, while also claiming the victories of what they have achieved in the past. "You don't let people write your history for you," advised Sonnenfeld, who is also the Lester Crown Professor of Management Practice as well as the founder and president of the Yale Chief Executive Leadership Institute. "You write it yourself."

By owning his past accomplishments, Neeleman is now the author of what he hopes to be his next tale of success at Azul. The only difficulty is that Neeleman, the father of nine children, including four who are still at home, spends four days a week in Brazil and then travels back to Connecticut to spend weekends with his family. It makes for quite a commute, which may prompt the Neeleman family to spend the North American summer in Brazil. But Neeleman seems happy with a career that spans the northern and southern hemispheres, because it allows him to do what he does best—run an innovative airline and serve others in the process. "I talk to people about it all the time," he said. "In Brazil, I talk to business leaders, to spread the Azul gospel, to get people to fly us and benefit from principles to have a better life."

Since his first big career upset when he was fired from Southwest Airlines half his lifetime ago, Neeleman has been recapturing success on his terms. Although he still feels the hurt of losing JetBlue, Azul has helped him move on. Neeleman's approach may not work for everyone; however, it is a formula for generating momentum that has carried him ahead into a promising future.

No matter how successful you are, there are always setbacks. Success in life demands the ability to bounce back.

—DAVID POTTRUCK,
FORMER CEO,
CHARLES SCHWAB & COMPANY

Chapter Two

DAVID POTTRUCK
A PORTRAIT IN CANDOR

G rowing up in the 1950s in a lower-middle-class neighborhood
on Long Island, David Pottruck never knew a business person.
All along the street where he lived as a young child were people who
worked in factories or in gas stations and bus drivers and policemen.
The only college graduate was a man on the corner who was a
teacher. Even without a role model, Pottruck, the oldest of four sons
in the family, dreamed big—beyond anything he knew or saw.

As Pottruck soon learned, aspirations alone could not take him
where he wanted to go. The only way to realize his goals was to
devote himself fully to the effort. "To be in the upper echelon, the
very top level, the effort to get there is extraordinary," Pottruck
explained. "It knows no boundaries. You are not only working
harder than everybody else, but a lot harder."

With unwavering resolve, Pottruck propelled himself from an
entry-level consulting job upward through the financial services
industry until he became CEO of Charles Schwab & Company. His
hard-charging attitude may have won the admiration of his bosses,
who recognized his talent and his ability to get results, but it did not
win him many friends among his peers. In fact, it would take years
for Pottruck to learn how collaboration could strengthen and grow
relationships.

With candor, Pottruck recounted the transformation in his life
as he reflected on the disappointments in his career and in himself.
Such honesty is uncommon in most people, but truly rare in a CEO,

who might be inclined to showcase accomplishments rather than emphasize failures.

Highly self-aware, Pottruck put into perspective his personal and professional life, including his twenty-year career with Charles Schwab & Company, during which he was steadily promoted until he became president, then co-CEO, and finally CEO. Then in 2004, with the brokerage industry still reeling from an economic downturn, he had to step down as CEO of Schwab. In order to move beyond the failure he felt, Pottruck had to draw upon all his previous experiences: a mixture of victories and defeats that he distilled into powerful lessons that have shaped his life and heightened his leadership.

Big Dreams and a Bright Beginning

For Dave Pottruck, both successes and disappointments came early. Among the top graduates in his high school class, Pottruck received awards for his academics and athleticism, which he hoped would earn him the scholarship he needed to attend a leading university. While many of his peers wanted to go to college, Pottruck had set his sights on an Ivy League school; achieving that goal would make him the first graduate of his high school to do so. Pottruck decided to attend the University of Pennsylvania, an elite and well-respected institution, which not only accepted him but offered a full scholarship. Penn was a good fit for Pottruck, who today expresses gratitude for his alma mater, from which both his daughter and stepdaughter have graduated and where his son is currently a student.

While at Penn, Pottruck majored in psychology and applied himself in athletics. He was named most valuable player of his football and wrestling teams, and rated All Ivy League in both sports. As graduation neared, Pottruck set another high goal for himself; this time, he wanted to play in the National Football League. His college coaches, however, did not share his enthusiasm. "They didn't see me as an NFL player. They weren't used to players aspiring to go to the NFL," Pottruck said. "Nobody pushed me in that direction."

That dream was not only lost when he wasn't picked in the NFL player draft, it later turned into bitter disappointment. In the fall of 1970 and a few months after his graduation from Penn, Pottruck learned that, in fact, he had been invited to try out as a free agent for the Miami Dolphins. Pottruck's letter of invitation from the Dolphins had been given to his wrestling coach, who put it in his desk and forgot about it for a few months. By the time Pottruck received the letter, the opportunity had passed. "The reason that story is particularly painful is that there was a guy from Amherst who played the same position I did and who was also invited to try out for the Dolphins. He started with the team and played in the Super Bowl. Perhaps that might have been me," Pottruck said.

Rather than wallow in disappointment, Pottruck channeled his energies in a new direction: getting a graduate degree in business from The Wharton School at the University of Pennsylvania. His career plan—driven by a desire, as he recalled, to "do good in the world"—was to go into hospital administration. His mother, no doubt, also influenced his choice. After marrying young, she attended college to earn her undergraduate and graduate degrees in nursing while Pottruck and his brothers were growing up.

His two years at Wharton provided not only a valuable education, but other learning experiences as well. While a graduate student, Pottruck took a job as an assistant coach for the college wrestling team at Penn. Suddenly he saw himself in these college athletes who had talent but didn't believe in themselves enough to become the best they could be. "They worked hard, but not hard enough to become an All-American or an Olympic athlete," Pottruck remembered. "This was an incredible, formative lesson at this stage of my life when I was twenty-two or twenty-three years old. If I wanted to be All-American in wrestling or an NFL football player, I had needed to train not just harder but much harder." His realization crystallized into a driving motivation to give his all to whatever opportunities materialized for him in the future.

Before graduating with an MBA in health administration, however, Pottruck would face one more disappointment. In addition to his studies at Wharton, he took pre-med classes, with the intention of adding a medical school degree to his MBA in health care administration. He applied to thirty schools, but was rejected. After working for a year in the health field, he applied to another twenty-two and made a few waiting lists, but in the end never was accepted. "Of course, things have worked out wonderfully since then. But back at this point in time, I was deeply humbled by this rejection," Pottruck observed.

As a young man, Pottruck was far more focused on his failures than on his successes. "Everybody around me was saying, 'Look at all you've accomplished, how fabulously you're doing! Why do you focus on what you haven't accomplished, not on what you have?'" Pottruck recalled. "I think I have tortured myself instead of enjoying what I have. I'm trying to learn that now."

By the mid-1970s, as Pottruck entered the business world for the first time, he took with him the sum of all his experiences, including the defeats and setbacks he had encountered already as a student and athlete. The lesson he had taken to heart above all was that he needed to work harder than anyone else if he wanted to succeed "in a spectacular fashion." As he observed, "I wanted to have a great career, so I would work at a high level of intensity, and that would make up for any lack of talent or experience. My ambition was very high."

Welcome to the Business World

With football and medical school now dead-end dreams, Pottruck focused on the opportunity before him: a job in 1974 in the consulting division of Arthur Young & Company, an accounting firm that later became Ernst & Young. Two years later, he joined

Citibank as a division controller at a time the bank was growing rapidly. "I didn't start on the ground floor; I was two levels below that," Pottruck laughed, recalling that his first office was on "sub-basement B" of Citibank's headquarters in New York.

Pottruck didn't stay in the bowels of the building for long. He was quickly promoted to run one of the accounting and technology functions for the bank. "I was managing huge projects and a data center, overseeing some of the programming and accounting operations," he recalled. "This was a time when a disk drive was the size of a washing machine and had memory storage that was less than that of a cell phone today." Even though the technology he was exposed to at the time would quickly become obsolete, he gained basic knowledge and developed important skills that would prove valuable throughout his career.

His next job at Citibank was in a regional mortgage and personal line of credit division, which he was eventually promoted to run. Pottruck, who had to take on marketing responsibilities as part of leading the division, quickly discovered he had a natural affinity for developing messages and campaigns that appealed to customers. After mastering his Citibank job, by the late 1970s Pottruck was looking for the next opportunity to advance his career and make more money. A call from a recruiter opened the door to Shearson, a brokerage firm that had just been purchased by American Express.

Pottruck joined Shearson as the head of marketing for retirement products such as individual retirement accounts, which put him in close contact with Joseph Plumeri, a well-regarded financial services executive who headed all marketing and sales promotions for Shearson at the time. "Joe and I had a real connection," Pottruck remembered. "Some other people were not performing and I was. In my first year, I was promoted twice."

With Plumeri championing him, Pottruck branched out from marketing retirement products into also marketing mutual funds, mortgages, and certificates of deposit. "I was working 100 hours a day," he described, but his efforts were paying off in terms of results. "The great thing about marketing is that, if you deliver value, your numbers go up. It can't be missed. The entire business goes through the marketing guy."

A fast rise in the company, a strong drive to succeed, and a brusque manner did not make Pottruck popular with many of his peers who saw him as an outsider from the banking industry, which was viewed as a world separate from brokerage. "For a long time, I was not a member of the club. I got promoted again, until I was doing all the consumer marketing and advertising for the company. Joe (Plumeri) would say, 'Hey you, Dave, you're my guy. You're not qualified on paper, but I know you can do this.'"

As the head of all consumer marketing and advertising at Shearson, Pottruck produced the results, but admitted he lacked the "political skills" that would have won him more supporters among his peers. "I was a bull in a china shop, a hard-working guy and somewhat intimidating. I had great support from the people who worked for me, and I had incredibly supportive bosses. Those who were my peers couldn't stand me. Partially it was because I was so successful that I was threatening. But a lot of it was because I was a jerk," he admitted. "But I never let that bother me at the time because I was so driven. It was not a good thing. Later, it came back to haunt me."

Today, Pottruck sees himself for who he is, who he was, and how far he has come. "If I had to do it over with what I know today, I would try to be more diplomatic. I produced incredible results, but I needed to be more embracing of others," he said. "I gave credit to my staff in those days, but not to a lot of other people."

During his years at Shearson, however, Pottruck could only see the facts at hand: he had climbed the ladder while being regarded as an outsider at the firm. In order to take his career to the next level, Pottruck knew he would have to go elsewhere.

By the end of 1983 and the beginning of 1984, change was afoot in the brokerage business, including the proliferation of discount commissions and greater participation by retail investors. When a recruiter approached Pottruck with a job opportunity to head the marketing division of Charles Schwab & Company, he was intrigued even though it meant relocating his family from New York to California. At the time, Schwab was a far smaller firm than the mega-brokerage houses, with only $100 million in revenue. Schwab, however, was taking a lead in discount brokerage, and Pottruck was interested in becoming part of the company, which was then owned by BankAmerica Corporation.

Joining Schwab brought Pottruck many new opportunities, but he did not change the way he operated. "I was the same guy, the same pluses and minuses followed me. Bosses liked me. Subordinates liked me. Peers could not stand me. I was incredibly effective and very successful, but there was broken glass everywhere—especially with my peers," Pottruck said.

Fortunately for him, Pottruck had a powerful ally in his corner: company founder Charles "Chuck" Schwab, who recognized his talent as well as his shortcomings. "He protected me," Pottruck added. "He knew how difficult I was to work with at the time."

Even though Chuck Schwab would later be the one to cause the biggest upset in his career, to this day Pottruck regards his former boss with great admiration and affection. "He considered me a trusted colleague. We had a great relationship and fun together, working arm in arm for twenty years," Pottruck remembered. "He was always in my corner, helping me with guidance and counsel. He was the most influential person of my entire career."

During Pottruck's first year at Schwab, the head of the branch network left the company. When that opportunity opened up, Pottruck made a pitch for the job and was promoted. The company, too, was undergoing change. In early 1987, BankAmerica sold Schwab back to Chuck Schwab. In September 1987, Charles Schwab & Company became publicly traded through an initial public offering.

Pottruck continued to rise through the ranks at Schwab, by the late 1980s becoming president of the brokerage operation, which accounted for about 90 percent of the company. The move promoted Pottruck into the inner circle of Schwab management, along with Larry Stupski, president and chief operating officer, and Chuck Schwab, who was chairman and CEO.

Although they established rapport as colleagues, Pottruck and Stupski were very different in style and demeanor, which set the stage for clashes between the two men. By 1990, Pottruck had decided that the best way to deal with their conflict was to move on, which he had done at other companies after a few years. When Chuck Schwab heard that Pottruck was interviewing with competitors, he called him into his office. His message, as Pottruck recalled, was simple and direct. "He said, 'I need you, Dave, to work with Larry, and I need Larry to work with you.'"

Pottruck agreed to stay and to work things out with Stupski. As he did, support came from an unlikely source: the therapist he was seeing while going through a divorce from his second wife. "My therapist said, 'I have good news and bad news. The good news is I am not convinced that you have a wife-selection problem. The bad news is I think you have a husband behavior problem,'" Pottruck recalled. The problem, as the therapist saw it, was a lack of partnership and collaboration. Pottruck quickly drew a parallel to his business relationships as well. "My idea at the time was that efforts to promote collaboration simply resulted in conflict. I couldn't see that it didn't have to be that way."

Heeding this wake-up call, Pottruck vowed to change his behavior, knowing it would be a long process and not at all easy. By being honest with himself and with others, he was determined to make the necessary breakthroughs both professionally and personally, since the two parts of his life were inextricably tied. "I was really committed to it," Pottruck said. "I began making the necessary attitude and behavioral adjustments. But it wasn't easy and real progress was slow."

Terry Pearce, a leadership communications consultant in the San Francisco area, worked closely with Pottruck starting in the early 1990s and later coauthored a book with him. As he sees it, Pottruck's commitment to authenticity not only helped his relationships with people, but also enhanced his leadership, enabling him to build greater rapport with others, who were more willing to follow him and trust his decisions. "Dave knew that trustworthiness was what was missing with some of his peers. He also learned that authenticity was key to changing their perception. He didn't have to give up his incredible intellect, but he could appeal to others not only through their minds, but also through their imaginations and their hearts," Pearce added.

The more self-reflective Pottruck became the more adept he was in expressing his thoughts and emotions even in a business context—as Pearce described it, "to show the math of what was going on inside him. This revelation made it possible for Dave's natural empathic nature to show up, and it changed his relationships."

In particular, Pottruck changed his interactions with Stupski during executive team meetings. Up to that point, Pottruck admitted, every meeting turned into a debate, with him on one side and Stupski on other. "Whatever he wanted to do, I thought I had a better idea. I realized I couldn't behave like that anymore."

He presented a solution to Stupski: He would no longer speak up in meetings when he disagreed with a plan or idea. Instead, they would discuss the matter privately. "Larry said, OK, you have a deal. That changed everything about the way we worked," Pottruck recalled. After that, the executive team meetings became more cohesive and productive, and differences between the two men were worked out in private and presented to the group as adjustments to the plan. "I never worried about who got the credit for any idea I brought to him," he added. "It was a way for me to grow emotionally. I was less concerned with the credit and more focused on the team being successful."

Through much of 1991 Pottruck mended fences at work, assuring colleagues that he had turned a new leaf and truly wanted to become a better partner. When he encountered people who remained skeptical, Pottruck asked that they only give him a chance. It was smoother sailing for Pottruck in his interaction with Stupski, which improved the dynamic of the executive team. Then an unexpected upset hit the team. Stupski had a heart attack, stepped down as president and chief operating officer of Schwab, and later retired. Pottruck was asked to take his position.

It was 1992 and Pottruck, who was forty-two years old, was now president of the entire company, but without the colleague on whom he had come to rely so heavily. "I didn't have Larry around to help me the way he used to. Instead of just following my instincts, I needed to become more disciplined, thoughtful, and meticulous in my approach. My code words to myself were, 'How would Larry do this?' I set about becoming a better version of Larry and me," he reflected.

While Pottruck was undergoing personal transformation, the company was posting very strong growth. In 1990, Charles Schwab & Company had customer assets (money that customers had in their accounts at the company) of $31 billion. By 1995, customer assets had risen to $182 billion, an incredible rate of 42 percent per year.[1] Growth was propelled by Schwab's industry-leading innovations: an "open architecture" no-load mutual fund marketplace that did not charge fees when investors put money into various third-party funds, and the development of a specialized service to support registered investment advisors (RIAs) who provided financial advice to retail customers.

The Internet opened the information superhighway to investors and provided access to investing online, thus sparking fundamental change in the way the brokerage business operated. In their book *Clicks and Mortar: Passion Driven Growth in an Internet Driven World*, Pottruck and Pearce chronicled the magnitude of that change. "By the winter of 1995, we knew that there were more computers being sold in the United States than television sets. This was an important turning point . . . ," they wrote. The Internet offered a perfect system for the financial services industry to create an explosion in online trading and investing. "If it [the Internet] was ever to be secure, it could represent one of the greatest breakthroughs in our business since the inception of the first stock market."[2]

In October 1995, e.Schwab, was launched, appealing to computer-savvy investors who needed little or no telephone-based customer service. By the end of 1995, 15 percent of Schwab's 15 million transactions originated from personal computers. The e.Schwab group started out as a small operation within the company that was "nimble, unshackled from the larger bureaucracy," Pottruck recalled at the time. Within a few years, as the online service became more popular, e.Schwab had to be integrated within the larger company.[3]

There were other changes in Pottruck's world in 1995: he and his current wife, Emily Scott, were married in May of that year. "Emily says I'm still a work in progress," Pottruck joked. "She has been an incredible partner for me." Happy in his personal life and with the business growing exponentially thanks to online trading, Pottruck seemed to have everything he wanted.

Things would only get better: online investing exploded in the brokerage industry and particularly at Schwab. Between December 1997 and December 1998, Schwab's online accounts rose from 1.2 million to 2.2 million, representing 40 percent of the company's accounts. The average number of daily trades rose 49 percent during the same period, with online trades accounting for 61 percent of the trading volume. With more assets under management and greater volume of trades, revenues also rose, increasing by 19 percent during 1998.[4]

Pottruck was understandably pleased with everything that had been accomplished at Schwab, but also recognized that it was time for the next challenge: specifically to become a CEO. In 1998, he had a conversation with Chuck Schwab, telling him of his plans. He wasn't asking for Schwab's job, Pottruck said; rather he wanted to start the process of identifying who would replace him. Schwab, who was sixty-one years old at the time, wanted to pursue a solution that would keep Pottruck with the company and enable him to become a CEO. After weighing various options, including making Pottruck CEO immediately, Schwab's proposal was for them to act as co-CEOs.

As he thought over Schwab's offer, Pottruck consulted with his wife, Emily, who encouraged him to give the arrangement a try. After all, he loved the company and did not want to leave, and he had a trusting relationship with Chuck Schwab. If it didn't work out, he could go on to something else.

Often, co-CEO arrangements become unworkable: two personalities and two management styles end up rupturing even the most well-intentioned partnership. Not so for Schwab and Pottruck, who had always enjoyed a good working relationship. "Chuck was the founder of the company. He was always going to be the icon, the guy who the press wanted to talk to. His name was on the door," Pottruck explained. "I was fine with that. He was the senior partner, and I was the junior. I would do the heavy lifting behind the scenes and Chuck would be the most visible."

Starting in 1998, Pottruck and Schwab were co-CEOs at a time of tremendous growth in the financial services industry, as online trading created a new type of retail investor: computer savvy and active. As *Fortune* magazine observed, "As the first company to figure out Internet trading, Schwab accommodated and spurred the frenzy and became the unofficial capital of Trader Nation."[5] Schwab expanded in online trading as a roaring bull market in the late 1990s fueled the explosion in day-trading and speculation in technology and Internet stocks.

A high point came in 2000 when Schwab had more than 13 million accounts and estimated that it was saving more than $100 million per year from its online trading service.[6] In February 2000, the company's Web site, Schwab.com, won the Enterprise Value Award from *CIO Magazine*, in recognition of how the company had used information technology to create fundamental change. Also that year, Pottruck and Schwab as co-CEOs shared the honor of being named the first "CEOs of the Year" by Morningstar, Inc., an award established to recognize leaders who maximize shareholder value and demonstrate independent thinking. Pottruck was further honored by being named by Congress to be a commissioner on the Advisory Commission on Electronic Commerce. *Information Week* also named him "CEO of the Year." The company had huge momentum, and Pottruck and Schwab were at the helm as the firm enjoyed one success after another.

The rapid pace of growth that Schwab and the rest of the brokerage industry had experienced through online trading could only continue for so long, particularly as the bull market in stocks ran out of steam. Soon, the bursting of a stock market bubble and a decline in online trading would translate into tough times for the entire financial services business. For Pottruck, there would be personal disappointment as well.

The Game Changes

Dot-com fever—the rapid expansion in the price of Internet-related stocks that saw three- and fourfold growth and sometimes more—helped propel the overall stock market even higher. By March 2000, the rise in stock market, driven partly by speculation, came to an end. When the stock market dropped sharply, the shares of high-flying technology and Internet companies were hit the hardest. The brokerage business suffered as retail investors realized later in 2000 and into 2001 that the game had changed.

"Schwab's customers went into shock," *Fortune* reported. The average daily number of trades rose from 28,000 in 1993 to 242,000 by the end of 2000. But by February 2001, average daily trades were down by half that amount.[7]

In the company's 2001 annual report, Pottruck told shareholders, "Obviously, we're disappointed with the kind of year we had financially in 2001." He acknowledged the "enormous competition" that Schwab faced, stating, "We're getting deeper into the business of giving advice, and that means we compete with everyone, from deep discount brokers to traditional full-service firms." Schwab had several advantages on its side, as Pottruck saw it: the world's largest online broker, the largest service provider to independent investment managers, and a leading distributor of third-party mutual funds.[8]

What everyone hoped would be a transition in the industry dragged on. Pottruck recalled 2000, 2001, and 2002 as tough years of layoffs and cutbacks at the company. Seeing himself as a builder, not someone who enjoys the challenge of downsizing, Pottruck found these tasks to be particularly difficult. Through the experience he learned a lot about himself; especially that his greatest strengths were in creating companies—not in cost-cutting and scaling back. In fact, during these difficult years Pottruck refused to accept bonuses from the company, believing that if employees who were hired during his watch needed to be let go then he shouldn't receive a bonus. Unfortunately, the entrenchment would continue for another year, only this time Pottruck would be alone at the helm.

In 2003, Chuck Schwab decided to turn all the reins over to Pottruck, making him the sole CEO while Schwab remained chairman. A Wall Street analyst, commenting on the move, told the *New York Times* that "Pottruck has been taking on more and more responsibilities for years. He had a big role in growing the business and will have an even more challenging job now in reviving the company's fortunes."[9]

While Pottruck continued to downsize the firm, he hoped to find another way to move the company forward with new growth. "I tried to cut as little as I could. I was trying to find a marketing solution to our problem, when the only solution was more cost reduction," he explained. In hopes of spurring some growth, in 2003 Pottruck led Schwab to acquire the institutional research and brokerage firm SoundView Technology. But the $321 million purchase price may have been too much. When the acquisition didn't work out as planned, the board began to lose confidence in his leadership.

As any CEO knows, tenure at the top can be brief. It's not uncommon for a CEO to be in place for only a few years before circumstances—from an earnings disappointment to a need to pursue another strategic direction—results in a management shakeup. By early 2004, Pottruck was aware that Schwab had had "three mediocre years in a row," and if things did not turn around soon there would be calls for him to be replaced. He recalled approaching Chuck Schwab about that possibility. "I told him, 'If that happens, don't toss me out like an old shoe. Let me know and we'll work out a transition.'" Chuck Schwab's response, as Pottruck recalled, was, "Dave, you've worked here twenty years. I would never do that you."

However, in July 2004, only a few months after that conversation, Chuck Schwab and a board member met with Pottruck, telling him it was time to resign. "I was not shocked professionally; I knew the company wasn't doing well. But I was personally devastated," Pottruck recalled.

Instead of couching the news in language about "leaving for personal reasons" Pottruck wanted the company announcement to reflect the truth: he had been asked to resign and was doing so reluctantly. He told the *New York Times* that the board's action came as a surprise, but that he accepted it. "Our performance since 2001 has been pretty lackluster," he added.[10]

Looking back, Pottruck remembers the feeling of "unmitigated humiliation" for not having the opportunity, at the age of fifty-six, "to do a year-end transition, to retire and be honored and leave with grace after twenty years." There would be no celebration at the end of his career at Schwab, only the feeling of defeat.

Bouncing Back

Pottruck did not wake up the morning after leaving Schwab with a new plan. Truth be told, he wasn't sure what he would do. What he did know was that he would eventually recover. In the interim, however, Pottruck dealt with feelings of public embarrassment. "A huge number of people in the world knew I had lost my last job," he explained.

A few days after he left Schwab, Pottruck received unwavering and much-appreciated support from Andy Grove, who was then Chairman of Intel Corp., where Pottruck has been a board member since 1998. "Andy came up to me and said, 'Are you a different man than you were two or three days ago? You lost your job but you are the same person. Nothing has really changed in that regard. We are delighted to have you on our board. To us, you are the same high-quality individual you were two or three days ago before you got fired.' His comments helped me tremendously."

Although he entertained thoughts of pursuing a high-level executive position with another firm, Pottruck knew that doing so would probably mean leaving California. "I just wasn't willing to make those sacrifices," he recalled. "I already had the best financial services job in the world, in the best company in the industry. Anything else just couldn't compare."

Pottruck recalled a seminal moment in his decision to put his personal life first, ahead of business, when his twenty-five-year-old son, Craig, approached him to discuss why he had cancelled their plans to get together. In the past, Craig had let it slide when his father's busy schedule prevented them from seeing each other. Father and son had a good relationship, and Pottruck had become much more emotionally available to his family. But when Pottruck fell into an old habit of cancelling plans because of a conflict, Craig confronted him. "When you were running Schwab, you cancelled things any number of times, and I always cut you slack," Craig told him. "You had thousands of people working for you then, but you don't have that any more. You haven't changed your behavior. I'm still at the back of the pack of your priorities."

His son's comments hit home hard. Pottruck immediately apologized to his son and took accountability for his actions, instead of making excuses. "I said to him, 'You are right. I am so sorry. I guess my habits are hard to change. I am so glad you called me on this, and I hope you will give me another chance.'" After working "100 hours a day," Pottruck woke up to the reality that he had to make up to his family for all the times he was unavailable to them. "I have changed since then," he added.

Pottruck was able to make significant changes in his personal and business life only because of his self-awareness. Self-knowledge has helped him to develop the emotional resilience necessary to process the defeats and savor the victories without losing sight of who he is as a person. As Terry Pearce observed, "It became a way of life. Dave was able to take the good with the bad with a lot of equanimity. When you can do that, things come and go, but they do not affect who you are. You can take a lot of negativity in your life with peace of mind. You do the best with what happens. It's not that you're saying, 'It doesn't matter.' It does matter. But you don't take it so seriously. You become more curious, wondering, 'How is this going to contribute to my life and create more opportunity?'"

Pottruck also came to appreciate how hard it must have been for Chuck Schwab—his friend, colleague, and boss for so many years—to tell him that he had to resign. "I never believed that Chuck intended to treat me badly. He always had been my protector," Pottruck reflected. "When I look at my life, I know that Chuck Schwab supported me for twenty years. I am incredibly grateful to him." With the passage of time, Pottruck also found consolation in the belief that he had enjoyed "a great nineteen years and fifty weeks at Schwab—and two bad weeks."

Once that chapter was over, Pottruck was committed to achieving greater balance in his life. He decided to forego another full-time senior executive position in favor of becoming involved on a part-time basis with a private equity firm that owned an all-first-class airline with service between New York and London. The airline, called Eos, was being run by a young CEO who had founded the firm. Pottruck was asked to become chairman and coach the

CEO. Although he was not familiar with the airline industry, Pottruck knew sales and marketing, and thought the campaign for Eos's launch was a disaster.

"I told the CEO, we're going to have empty planes. He blew me off," Pottruck recalled. "The airline launched, and the planes were empty. After five weeks of burning through millions of dollars, the board came to me and asked if I would take over as CEO and run the airline on an interim basis until a new CEO could be found."

Rather than take the CEO job right away, Pottruck decided to assume the title of executive chairman, which connoted more of an advisory role, although soon he was running the airline. He set an ambitious goal: before the airline ran out of money in four months, it would prove to be viable. Working a few days a week in New York and the rest of the time in California, Pottruck oversaw operations, insisting on using daily metrics that measured how well the airline was performing, such as the number of passengers per day and the number of newly booked reservations. Within its first year, Eos had largely turned around, filled its first daily flight, launched a second flight between New York and London, and was able to raise another $75 million. While the company was seeking investor capital, Pottruck had to step in officially as the CEO of the airline.

Sounding very much like the avid athlete Pottruck has been all his life, he likened turning around the situation at Eos to skiing a "double black diamond course—as tough as it gets." He explained, "I didn't know the airline business. They were going to shut us down. Think about the morale among the pilots and the flight attendants as they were staring at empty jets every day. I stepped in, the non-airline guy, and tried my best to get everybody excited again about the very special kind of airline we wanted to build."

Eos reached two important milestones during Pottruck's brief tenure as CEO: the company approached flight level breakeven on an operating basis, and it was named the 2007 Business Travel World "Long-Haul Business Airline of the Year," an impressive feat for a new airline. In 2007, Pottruck decided it was time to declare victory and pass the baton to someone else. After Pottruck left, Eos continued to expand until it reached four or five flights a day and was planning to add additional routes. When oil prices spiked over $150 a barrel in 2008, the airline was saddled with high fuel costs and started to lose significant amounts of money. Eventually, it ceased operation.

Pottruck considers Eos a disappointment as a new venture investment, but a shot-in-the arm of confidence for him. "I needed to look in the mirror and know that I was authentically capable and could go into a situation and use all the skills I had developed at Schwab to build something and fulfill an exciting vision," he added.

Today, Pottruck is devoting almost all of his professional time as co-chairman of the board of HighTower, a private equity-backed, high-net-worth wealth management firm. Pottruck spoke enthusiastically about this new venture, where he works closely with the firm's executive team "raising money, recruiting new advisors, and helping to build the culture and the team."

But not all of Pottruck's time is spent in business. Pottruck also teaches at the Wharton School, which enables him to share his experiences with students. Another very important focus is philanthropic activity, especially providing support for foster children for whom he feels particular passion. "The foster care system is horribly broken," he said. "These kids can succeed and they desperately need our support. With a modest amount of money we can change lives for the better."

He and his wife are committed to other organizations, including the U.S. Olympic Team, U.S. Ski Team, Jewish charities, V-Day, which seeks to stop violence against women and girls, the Park City, Utah, Community Foundation, and Emily's alma mater, Simmons College, and of course, his—Penn. Among Pottruck's many gifts to Penn has been the David S. Pottruck Health and Fitness Center, a facility that is adjoined to the school's Gimbel Gymnasium. In an interview with the *Daily Pennsylvanian*, Pottruck quipped that although his family's legacy to the university has been to provide an array of scholarships and endow a faculty chair, "I think we'll forever be known as the people who gave the gym."[11]

Pottruck is comfortable with the realization that he no longer needs to pursue a big CEO job to set things right in his life. The sting he felt so sharply from being asked to resign is fading. He now has a life he truly loves. "All these jobs—the power, the money, and the leadership—they are intoxicating," he said. "It's very easy to believe that you have to have that rush, that power. But you don't. It comes with the huge cost of consuming your energy and much of your life. You can have an incredible opportunity to mold your life in a different direction, although it's not easy at first to accept that. But you can redefine success after an experience like that."

His advice for those who are in the midst of a career upset, regardless of what their future plans might hold, is to acknowledge the talents, abilities, and experiences that contributed to their careers in the past. "The things that made you successful before can make you successful again," he added.

Even his final disappointment of leaving Schwab has not kept Pottruck from viewing his leadership at the company—starting when he was promoted to president of the firm—as the most proud accomplishment of his professional life. "I ran Schwab for twelve years as Chuck's partner," he said. "We built a helluva company."

Beyond his steely resolve and commitment to work harder than anyone else, Pottruck's success has as much to do with recovering from defeats and disappointments as it does with building on accomplishments. The journey has not been easy at times, but through it he has learned a powerful lesson: "No matter how successful you are, there are always setbacks. Success in life demands the ability to bounce back."

The self-knowledge that Pottruck has gained and the candor with which he shares it are priceless. By owning everything he has experienced, Pottruck has become an authentic leader, capable of truly inspiring others through his story, while investing in the relationships and the activities in his life that matter the most to him.

[People] rallied around me—literally and figuratively. I got hundreds of e-mails from people I worked with and for; clients and employees and people who had been my bosses . . . that made a huge difference. If the world had gone silent, I would have been devastated.

—PATRICIA DUNN,
FORMER CHAIRMAN OF THE BOARD,
HEWLETT-PACKARD CORPORATION

Chapter Three

PATRICIA DUNN
TRIAL BY FIRE

P atricia Dunn's career was a Cinderella tale in the hard-core world of financial services, rising from humble beginnings to become CEO of the world's largest institutional investment management firm, Barclays Global Investors. Dunn prided herself on having built impeccable integrity and trustworthiness over the years, until she was ultimately responsible for overseeing nearly a trillion dollars in client assets. For the woman who started her career "at the bottom of the bottom" as she described, it was an extraordinary and impressive accomplishment.

Gracious and understated, Dunn earned the respect of her peers in the male-dominated financial services industry. Beyond her own accomplishments, Dunn was also credited with attracting a very talented, high-performing team. In short, Dunn was widely admired for her professionalism, integrity, and fair-mindedness. It would seem implausible, if not completely impossible, that her reputation would later be on the line over the handling of an internal investigation at computer giant Hewlett-Packard Corporation, where she had been a board member and was then asked to become chairman. Suddenly Dunn was on the firing line, facing allegations that were in direct contrast with everything she had stood for in her career. Throughout it all, Dunn maintained her innocence and her composure while dealing with a hostile media, vicious detractors, and state, federal, and Congressional investigations.

Reflecting on the entire ordeal, Dunn never raised her voice or expressed any bitterness. She recounted with quiet eloquence the battles she waged, including against a serious threat to her health. Through it all, she exemplified the qualities that people ascribe to her: thoughtful, attentive, and without ego. Enduring a trial by fire, Dunn learned deeply powerful lessons grounded in self-knowledge and what, in the end, really matters.

Dunn's career at Barclays and her chairmanship at Hewlett-Packard were a long way from where she started. She grew up in Las Vegas, where her father, who died when Dunn was eleven, was the entertainment director at the Dunes and the Tropicana Hotels. As a student at the University of California, Berkeley, which she attended on scholarships, Dunn had wanted to pursue a journalism career. After she graduated in December 1975 opportunity knocked elsewhere: a job as a temporary secretarial assistant for Wells Fargo Investment Advisors starting in January 1976. Dunn laughed as she recalled that when the temporary agency called with the Wells Fargo assignment, her mother accepted it on her behalf without even discussing the job with her.

"I had very little thought of making Wells Fargo my career. But despite my initial bias against finding anything worthwhile in that assignment, I came into contact with some incredibly smart, interesting people who were on a mission: to revolutionize the world of investment management, which was riddled with in-efficiency and high costs," Dunn explained.

With a keen mind and a talent for writing, Dunn soon began working with the marketing department, where she was able to translate financial lingo into plain, understandable English. After two years in a supposedly temporary assignment, Dunn had to make a choice: become a permanent employee, which Wells Fargo urged her to do, or leave. Although financial services had not been her first choice in a career, the decision was an easy one to make. "By that time," she said, "I was hooked."

Once she made the decision to stay with Wells Fargo, Dunn's career ascent was swift and impressive. Her first appointment into the lower level of management was becoming an assistant vice president in 1980. In those days, investment management was far smaller in scale than it is today, which provided Dunn the opportunity to be involved in a variety of functions, including operations, administration, portfolio management, trading, client relations and client services, and sales. She held a number of positions in those functions before joining the firm's senior management team in the mid-1980s.

Meanwhile, Wells Fargo Investment Advisors was going through major growth and global expansion. In the early 1980s, Wells Fargo had spun off the investment management business as a 100 percent-owned subsidiary. Then, in the late 1980s, as operations expanded overseas and Japan was the fastest growing market, Wells Fargo sold half of the investment management unit to a Japanese financial services company. As the company grew, so did Dunn's responsibilities. In 1994, she was appointed president of the firm, and then in January 1997 was made co-chairman with Fred Grauer, an early convert from academia to quantitative investing, enabling them to split responsibilities by geography and function. It was time for another change as the joint venture with the Japanese partner ended and Wells Fargo sold the business to Barclays. The firm then became Barleys Global Investors.

In mid-1998, Grauer left Barclays and Dunn became the sole chairman and CEO. Rising to the top of one of the most respected financial services firms was quite an accomplishment, particularly for a woman in the 1990s. Dunn may have lacked the Ivy League business school pedigree of some of her C-suite peers, but there was no deficit when it came to her intelligence, grasp of the industry, and strategic vision. But even then Dunn did not see herself or what she had accomplished as extraordinary. More on her mind was the job at hand, which was enormous. "I don't think

I felt that sense of having achieved an apex at the time. Looking back, it's easier to see," she commented. "At the time, I felt a tremendous sense of responsibility and a healthy amount of fear. Fear of failure is an underrecognized motivator. The business was like having a tiger by the tail—incredibly fast-growing. I was more focused on managing the growth and taking advantage of the opportunities."

As an institutional investment manager, Barclays Global Investors handled pensions for firms such as Boeing, General Electric, and SONY. One of Dunn's most notable accomplishments as CEO, however, was expanding the company into the retail sector with a new product: iShares, helping to innovate the industry's fastest-growing new product, exchange-traded funds (ETFs). ETFs date back to the late 1980s and allow investors to buy shares in an index—such as the Standard & Poor's 500, an industry sector such as technology or health care, or even a particular foreign market—with lower fees and at any time of day, just like a stock. By contrast, mutual funds can only be traded once a day. Barclays Global Investors launched a predecessor ETF in 1996 with a product known as World Equity Benchmark Shares or WEBS. Later, that product became iShares, which Barclays introduced in the United States and Canada in 2000. With that rollout, Dunn was in the spotlight in the investment industry. As a *BusinessWeek* article noted at the time: "She's serious about putting BGI [Barclays Global Investors] on the retail fund market map for good . . . Dunn has been moving the Old Economy BGI toward a New Economy frontier: . . . The industry may not like it, but Dunn's noisy entry into the mainstream has changed the rules. Like Dunn, ETFs will make a lasting imprint."[1]

Under Dunn's leadership, Barclays Global Investors became the world's largest player in ETFs. It also dominated as the largest institutional fund manager in the world, managing collective assets such as public pension funds, corporate pension funds, 401(k) plans, sovereign government funds, and funds from endowments and foundations. When the federal government in 2006 expanded investment offerings under its Thrift Savings Plan, a retirement plan for federal employees, which as of mid-2008 had more than $230 billion in assets, Barclays Global Investors was among the contenders to manage the equity portion of the portfolio. "It was one of the most highly contested assignments in the history of investment management," Dunn remembers proudly. Barclays won.

(In June 2009, Barclays Global Investors was purchased by BlackRock, Inc. for about $13.5 billion. At the time of the deal, Barclays Global Investors operated in fifteen countries and managed more than $1 trillion in assets.)

Meanwhile, Dunn's accomplishments attracted increasing media attention. In 1999, *Fortune* magazine had listed Patricia Dunn, then aged forty-six, as number eleven on its list of the "50 Most Powerful Women" for that year. The list contained a who's who of women in the corporate ranks. In the number one spot was Carly Fiorina, then CEO of Hewlett-Packard.

Reflecting on her leadership through her many years at Wells Fargo and then Barclays, Dunn emphasized the requisite qualities of trust, integrity, and accountability—not just for herself, but also for every person in the industry. "Everyone who is involved in fund management, whether retail or institutional, has a fiduciary responsibility. But that responsibility at Wells and then at Barclays seemed extraordinarily large," Dunn said. "I used to explain this to people all the time, especially new employees, what it meant to be a fiduciary of other people's money. It is doing for other people and their money what you would do it if were your own."

In 2005, while distinguishing herself at Barclays Global Investors, Dunn was about to take on another challenge—this time as nonexecutive chairman of the Hewlett-Packard board, which she had joined in 1998. Through that experience, Dunn would learn the toughest lessons when her leadership and her integrity were severely challenged.

Joining the HP Board

In 1998, while she was chairman and CEO of Barclays, Dunn was invited to become a director of Hewlett-Packard by then-CEO Lou Platt. A Hewlett-Packard director with an investment management background had left the board, and Platt wanted to replicate that expertise. Dunn brought to the board experience as a buyer of technology at Barclays Global Investors, as well as broad business knowledge such as treasury functions, risk management, audit functions, and hedging to mitigate currency fluctuations. Dunn's first board assignment was on the finance and investment committee.

In 1999, Platt was replaced as CEO by Carly Fiorina, who took on the chairman's title in 2000. In the earlier years of her tenure at Hewlett-Packard, Fiorina was praised for bringing flair to the "gray old lady" of Silicon Valley, but later she was criticized internally and externally for being unable to execute against a strategy to grow and compete against the likes of Dell and IBM. On January 24, 2005, the *Wall Street Journal* published a front page article, quoting anonymous sources who stated that the Hewlett-Packard board was dissatisfied with Fiorina's performance and had considered a management reorganization during a private retreat. That level of detailed information, it became clear to the company, could only have come from a board member or member of senior management who was leaking information to the press.[2] Such a breach of confidentiality violated the strict rules of conduct by which board members are bound and created an atmosphere of mistrust among directors that undermined the board's effectiveness. Hewlett-Packard had faced leaks for a few years, but the *Journal* article became a line in the sand, as it were, indicating just how far disclosure of unauthorized information to the media had gone and how damaging it could be for the company—and in particular a technology firm that thrives on innovation and strategy, which must be kept secret from competitors.

The *Journal* article proved correct. A month later, the board of directors asked Fiorina to resign. Robert P. Wayman, who had been the CFO for more than twenty years, became interim CEO until a new chief executive was hired. Dunn was asked by her board colleagues to serve as nonexecutive chairman. She was viewed as somewhat of a neutralizing force on the Hewlett-Packard board, which had become polarized over Fiorina. "I was the one person every member of the board was talking to at the moment." Dunn reasoned. "I was the least objectionable alternative that they could agree on." For Dunn, however, becoming chairman was not a position she sought out or wanted. In fact, she had strong reservations about taking the position. The need to act expediently, however, proved more compelling. "I was given a very clear message from the board that a decision had to be made immediately," Dunn recalled. "They did not want to go to the marketplace with an uncertain leadership structure. So I agreed to do it."

Dunn realized quickly that the position of chairman would be a thankless job at best and a no-win situation in the worst. "There was a faction of the board that—while they supported me as chairman—expected me to be completely compliant with their wishes, and another group that was sure this was the case and for whom I tried to work hard to assure that was not so," she explained. Aware of the difficulties the board was having working together, Dunn spoke with each director individually, in his or her home location, to draw out the issues and build bridges to resolve them. Given the fractious nature of the board, however, Dunn became doubtful that she or anybody else could successfully lead it.

In a quandary, Dunn sought the advice of a lawyer who, she said, had impeccable credentials in corporate governance and described the situation she faced with the board—including that she was considering stepping down as chairman. "He said to me, 'You were just elected two or three months ago. Your fiduciary responsibility is to the shareholders. You may not be able to solve the problems, but you have to give it your best shot. If you don't want to stand for election next year, fine. But it would be a violation of your fiduciary responsibility in spirit if you did not carry on and give it your best shot.' So I did. I thought that advice when I heard it sounded right."

Agreeing to stay on as chairman, Dunn pursued her top priorities, which were, first, to help recruit a permanent CEO for Hewlett-Packard and, second, to put a stop to information leaks that were plaguing the board. The leaks coming from the board of directors dogged Hewlett-Packard right into the appointment of a new CEO, Mark Hurd, who had spent twenty-five years at NCR Corp., the last two years as CEO. Before Hurd's announcement was made in March 2005—and before he had notified the NCR board—*BusinessWeek* had the story and called Hewlett-Packard for confirmation. "That was one of the issues causing the greatest distress," Dunn explained. "Everyone suspected everyone else. They wanted to know where [the leaks] were coming from."

As she would later explain in testimony before Congress, "The majority of directors told me during my first few weeks as chairman that, next to leading the board's CEO search, coming to grips with HP's famously leaky board should be my top priority. They were particularly disturbed because Carly Fiorina's attempt to do this in January 2005, through interviews conducted by outside counsel, had come to naught. Thus, directors knew that whoever was talking to the press was unwilling to come forward to make a clean breast of the matter. This served only to deepen mutual distrust. Identifying the source of leaks on the HP board was seen by many directors as 'unfinished business' from Ms. Fiorina's tenure as chairman."[3]

With the blessing of the board to find a way to plug the leaks, Dunn approached Hewlett-Packard's acting CEO for his input on the problem. He suggested that Hewlett-Packard's internal investigations unit was in a good position to carry out an investigation. Ultimately the investigation was turned over to the company's general counsel. No directors, including Dunn or members of executive management, were exempt from the investigation. In mid-2006, the investigation identified the leaker: board member

Jay Keyworth, who had run the physics division at the Los Alamos National Laboratory and had been the President's Science Advisor in the Reagan Administration, serving as principal architect of the "star wars" nuclear missile defense shield initiative."[4]

Faced with this information, Dunn convened a meeting of Hewlett-Packard's CEO, general counsel, senior outside counsel, and chairman of the board's audit committee for advice as to how to deal with the investigation's finding. "The opinion of this group was unambiguous, which was that the entire board had a right and a responsibility to decide what, if anything, should be done with the results of the investigation," she explained. It was agreed that the audit committee chairman would present the findings to the board and disclose the identity of the leaker. Later, Dunn reflected that if the advisory group she had convened decided not to reveal the leaker's identity to the board—"for the good of the company and the peace and tranquility of the board"—she would have gone along with the plan. "Maybe that would have blown up, too. There was no peaceful way out of this."

After the audit committee chairman presented the board with the results of the investigation, intense deliberations followed over what should be done. A motion was made to ask for Keyworth's resignation. When the motion passed, another board member, Tom Perkins, who was a friend of Keyworth's, resigned from the board. What followed, Dunn said, was a public-relations campaign launched by Perkins, which resulted in scathing media accounts "to make a public enemy out of me, to shame me, to see me punished." Dunn was in the crosshairs over the investigation, including the use of a tactic known as pretexting, whereby personal information such as phone records is obtained using the pretense of being someone else. The legal status of pretexting at the time was unclear but has since been outlawed. The uproar over the use of pretexting later led to an investigation by California state prosecutors.

Dunn maintained that her actions were in line with what any chairman would do under similar circumstances, and that at every turn she was assured that Hewlett-Packard's investigative techniques were fully compliant with applicable law. As she explained to Leslie Stahl in an interview on 60 *Minutes*, "If you think that Hewlett-Packard is the only company that has an investigations force you're being naïve. Every company has investigations. Investigations by their nature are intrusive."[5] Dunn firmly stated that she was not involved in the choice of investigative methods used. "I didn't hire anybody. I was a suspect. I was investigated. I was pretexted," she explained. "I never thought it was possible that there was anything going on [in the investigation] that wouldn't pass muster if it was published on the front page of the *New York Times*. But the only way to know that would have been to meddle in the investigation, which, as a subject, I didn't do."

Soon, it was Dunn's picture on the front page of newspapers and the covers of magazines across the United States, Europe, and Asia with damning headlines about the "corporate spying scandal" at Hewlett-Packard that the media compared to Watergate, and calling for Dunn's resignation.

Meanwhile the leaks continued as did the articles quoting "insiders" and board sources. A *BusinessWeek* article, written by a reporter who said he had been "pretexted" as part of the investigation, cited a source "familiar with the board's proceedings," who pushed for Dunn's resignation: "If she isn't canned the whole board is going to have to say that what happened wasn't so bad," the "insider" claimed.[6]

Pressure on Dunn escalated as California state prosecutors launched an investigation. In early September 2006 the California state attorney general had announced that pretexting violated two state laws, and was investigating whether criminal charges in the Hewlett-Packard case were warranted. Although Dunn would later be exonerated, first she would have to experience intense negative publicity as she was attacked in the media, in the state courthouse, and on Capitol Hill. If that were not enough, Dunn was also battling stage four ovarian cancer, enduring surgery and chemotherapy.

Embattled on Two Fronts

Through much of her ordeal at Hewlett-Packard Dunn was literally fighting for her life. In 2001, she had been diagnosed with breast cancer, followed by melanoma in 2002. In the midst of cancer treatments, Dunn had to step down as CEO of Barclays Global Investors in 2002, although she remained vice chairman of the firm. In 2004, she was diagnosed with stage four ovarian cancer. Then, in the late summer of 2005, Dunn underwent further surgery for a recurrence of ovarian cancer. As she waged her battles against the disease, Dunn exhibited a steely resolve that reflected the seriousness of what she faced.

"I came to a philosophical decision, if there is such a thing. It was way back in the earlier period of dealing with my diagnosis of ovarian cancer. I said, 'Okay, you're dead. Life is over for you. You have just pulled the black ball out of the urn of white balls. There is nothing you can do about it. So just come to terms with it.' And what happens then is you wake up and you feel good; it's a new day. And you go out and you do what you do, and enjoy the people you are working with and have time with your family. Every day is a bonus."

Dunn's ability to cope was grounded in her ability to look unflinchingly at reality instead of trying to convince herself that things were somehow different. "I figured out you just come to terms as quickly as possible with the worst-case scenario, and then everything else is upside," she added.

Dunn found, as many do who have a major and unexpected upset in their lives, that enduring a hard fall in one's life strips away the pretenses. From this willingness to look at the truth comes the strength and conviction to move forward; not to rebuild the past or reclaim the status quo, but to envision a different life from the pieces that remain. Out of this low point, one's natural creativity and resourcefulness become engaged. A kind of freedom sets in that allows a person to generate solutions and ways forward that could not be imagined when life was going smoothly.

Athena Katsaros, an executive coach and trainer specializing in leadership and life skills, calls this rock-bottom stage "the pit." It is the nadir in the development curve that she equates to the hero's journey—a term coined by mythologist Joseph Campbell that describes a sojourn that takes a person through upheaval and trauma to self-discovery and ultimately breakthrough to a higher place of awareness and possibility. Too often, however, the pit is where people give up because they tell themselves that they will never overcome the challenges that they are facing and find their way to being whole again. There are others like Dunn, however, who hit rock bottom and then successfully traverse to the other side because they keep trying to find a way forward, even as they confront the stark reality of the severity of their situations.

"People who make it through to the other side are the ones who don't give up. They have faith in themselves. Some may also look to the Universe or God to help them move through this challenging place. Inevitably they look at the deeper questions: including, 'What's important to me now? How am I willing to change? What am I not seeing? What do I need to let go of?'" Katsaros said.

In order to lift themselves up, Katsaros advised, people have to let go—particularly of old ideas about who they are and what their lives are about. "This is a powerful phase: it's a time in your life when you have to face the fact that what you thought you knew is no longer relevant and what you believed was solid ground is shifting beneath you. You find yourself in unknown territory without a map," she added. "You have to let go of expectations of how you think it all works and how it's supposed to be. When you have faith in yourself and your own innate creativity you will discover all kinds of un-expected strategies and solutions that will get you out of the pit."

As Dunn dealt with the need to mount a legal defense, dealing with cancer presented some unexpected advantages. "I really had only so many first-place enemies to be fighting," she recalled. She had to choose her battles, literally. First priority was cancer treatment to achieve a state of remission.

Meanwhile, the aftermath and press accounts of the Hewlett-Packard investigation became a surreal experience for Dunn. "I thought it was absurd . . . I guess there is a certain self-protective instinct that kicks in, that I couldn't believe that anybody whose opinion I cared about was going to be taken in by the ridiculousness of what was happening."

In the midst of the maelstrom of controversy swirling around her, Dunn received a very public show of support when she was chosen by the Bay Area Council to be inducted into its Hall of Fame in September 2006—a high honor and a rare achievement for a woman. "I was incredibly flattered. The people who are on the selection committee and on the council never wavered," Dunn recalled. "I got in touch with one of the members of the committee quietly and said, 'Look, I feel really bad for you guys that this is happening. I will totally understand if the decision is to withdraw my [induction] and no hard feelings.' He said, 'You've got to be kidding. The only conversation that we've had is, if we had to do it over again, we'd do exactly the same thing.'"

In remarks before an audience of 800 people, Dunn said she looked forward to having an opportunity to "set the record straight" regarding the Hewlett-Packard investigation and the allegations she was facing. She was given a standing ovation. According to press reports, the audience was largely supportive, and Dunn was called "courageous" for appearing at the event and "a very forthright person." Yet even in the midst of this honor, there was criticism. One article quoted an attorney who declined to be identified, who commented, "I think it's unbelievably arrogant of [the council] to select her when she is under an egregious cloud of suspicion."[7]

Days after the induction, Dunn resigned as chairman of Hewlett-Packard and, despite having surgery just weeks before, would be heading to Washington soon to appear before a Congressional panel that had launched its own inquiry into what was being called a case of corporate spying. As Dunn described in her Congressional testimony in September 2006, explaining why she resigned early from the chairman's post, she had become "a lightning rod for criticism for the company and the board." Although she had already decided to resign as chairman in January 2007, she agreed to do so sooner. "I left the board with good feelings, embraces, and clear messages from each director that they regretted that this had happened to me."[8]

The Accountability Conundrum

Given the ongoing criminal investigation, Dunn faced a difficult decision regarding testifying before Congress in late September 2006. Under the circumstances, Dunn could have asserted her rights under the Fifth Amendment to protect herself from self-incrimination. "My lawyer told me if I testified and there was an inadvertent discrepancy between what I said before Congress and what was in the thousands of documents surrounding the matter, none of which I had seen at that point, I could be completely innocent and still be charged with perjury," she said. "He told my husband that he would normally advise a client to take the fifth, as ruinous to one's reputation as it is. But he said in this case he thought I should testify if I wanted to."

In the end, Dunn chose to testify to speak the truth. "I was up for it. I was wishing, certainly, that it had never come to that. But I wanted to tell my story. I was getting mad."

Told to expect an hour of hearings, Dunn endured almost six hours of hostile questioning. "At that point, I thought it was a personal challenge," she said. "In the thousands of pages of documents that were subsequently part of the discovery for the case, there was apparently never any discrepancy found between what I prepared as written testimony and what I gave as oral testimony. I haven't gone through the documents. My husband has read every word many times. I don't have to look at them. I want to keep my memory unblemished."

One of the criticisms Dunn faced was that she never apologized or expressed any remorse publicly or in the media over what critics saw as her role in the investigation. Dunn learned that when people express regrets or accountability for others' actions that might involve crimes, they set themselves up as targets for prosecutors. "I believe in accountability. In fact, I made a video with Mark [Hurd] for the 32,000 HP employees globally and apologized for what had happened. When my lawyer found out I had done that, he said, 'What in the world were you thinking?' I said, 'These people work for HP. Their company's name is being dragged through the mud every day.'"

Dunn's sense of accountability was tempered by her lawyer's insistence that she not apologize in her Congressional testimony because she had, in fact, done nothing wrong. Dunn told her lawyer that then she would just be "another one of those assholes who said they did nothing wrong." Besides, Dunn added, she was innocent. "Innocent people go to jail all the time," her lawyer replied.

"Four hours into the questioning, a Congressman went off on a tirade and said, 'I didn't hear you take one ounce of responsibility. I haven't heard you accept accountability or make apologies. Don't you agree that you are culpable?'" Dunn recalled. "I said, 'Sir, I do not believe I am culpable.' He said, 'Then you should resign.' I told him, 'I did resign last week, but if you want me to do that again, I will.'"

On October 4, 2006—less than a week after Dunn testified in Washington—the California attorney general announced that Dunn and four people connected with the Hewlett-Packard investigation were being charged with four felonies: using false or fraudulent pretenses to obtain confidential information from a public utility, unauthorized access to computer data, identity theft, and conspiracy to commit each of those crimes. The charges carried the possibility of thousands of dollars in fines and a potential jail term.

To deal with the shock of the criminal allegations, Dunn relied on the continued goodwill of others around her who refused to believe that she was guilty. "I had to make a cosmic distinction between those I knew and didn't know, and those whose opinions matter to me and those I could never know and therefore what they thought was less important," she explained.

This ability to separate in her mind those who were in her camp and those whose opinion she could not influence enabled Dunn to maintain her footing through the difficult days and months ahead. Rather than being unnecessarily distracted by what she could not change, Dunn was able to face the challenges confronting her.

A lengthy feature in *The New Yorker* published in February 2007 on the Hewlett-Packard leak investigation painted clearly just how dire a situation Dunn faced. As the author wrote, "What started out on Dunn's part as a quest for higher ethical standards led to a lawless, out-of-control investigation and possibly a prison term."[9]

Dunn's legal battle finally came to an end in March 2007 when a judge dropped all charges against her, "in the interest of justice." A few weeks earlier, state prosecutors had offered to exchange the four felony charges for a guilty plea to one misdemeanor, which she refused. (Three other defendants entered no contest pleas to misdemeanor charges to avoid jail time.) "This is a vindication of Pattie Dunn in every sense of the word," Dunn's lawyer said in a CBS News article. "It shows what she's maintained throughout, that she's innocent of these charges."[10]

Dunn's exoneration made headlines, but not nearly to the degree of the very public flogging she had endured in the press. It was as if facing four felony charges and seeing her professional reputation dragged through the mud made Dunn more newsworthy than having the charges dismissed completely. Dunn, however, had her say in an interview with *Fortune* magazine that appeared two months after the charges were dropped. In it, she described the difficult times from surgery for cancer recurrence to dealing with charges filed against her in October 2006 and starting chemotherapy two days later. "I was pretty much grounded the whole time, except for going to Washington to testify before Congress.

I was recovering from surgery and also being hounded by the media. We were living in San Francisco at the time, and at one stage I didn't go out of my apartment for two-and-a-half weeks. Given that privacy was the core issue in the HP case, that was pretty ironic," Dunn told *Fortune*.

Asked if she felt defamed, Dunn said there was no doubt that she was. "Until this happened to me, I assumed that when a corporate executive was charged with a crime, they were guilty. So I assumed that everyone would think I was guilty."[11]

Lessons Learned

Dunn spoke candidly of the lessons she learned through her painful experiences, some specific to the Hewlett-Packard ordeal, and others of a more philosophic variety. Looking back, she concluded that "the biggest lesson was that there are some problems that you can't fix. This is not something that is [easy to accept] for anyone— especially if one spent a career in a leadership role in any capacity. We are all wired to succeed, to find a solution, to gain our success by being the people who figure out the problems. Our rewards are often to get bigger problems to solve."

Although she had some reservations taking on the chairman's post at Hewlett-Packard, Dunn said she had convinced herself that she would be the one to solve the problems. "There is a certain amount of ego that is encapsulated in that. Some of it is healthy, achievement-oriented stuff. Other parts are not so healthy," she said. "I think I overestimated my ability to solve the deep divisions that existed among this group of people. I thought if anyone could do it, I could do it. And I couldn't. I learned that lesson, which is that you need to know when to quit. It's not an easy or a happy lesson."

Dunn also stressed the importance of allies and supporters, starting with her husband, Bill Jahnke. Throughout the ordeal, family, friends, and business associates rallied around her. "I would feel very badly for anyone who goes into one of these personal crucibles at a point that they don't have a solid family situation. I think that would be a whole different kettle of fish, if they are going through a divorce or are estranged from family, unless they have some other meaningful support system," Dunn reflected.

Dunn remembered that throughout the ordeal she was incredibly well-supported, especially by her family. "They just had blind faith that whatever bad things were being said couldn't be true. I got so many demonstrations of their support during that period. It was almost overwhelming. They rallied around me— literally and figuratively. I got hundreds of e-mails from people I worked with and for; clients and employees and people who had been my bosses. I got so many messages from people saying, 'This is ridiculous. We know it can't be true—we know you. Ignore it. Be strong and don't let it get you down.' That made a huge difference. If the world had gone silent, I would have been devastated."

Knowing that she had done nothing wrong and buoyed by others, Dunn had a strong foundation on which to stand as she faced grueling adversity. Her mantra became "I know what I know," which applied in particular to what she did and didn't do as part of the investigation. Dunn acknowledged that there were plenty of people who believed she was guilty, including journalists whose slant is obvious when reading the articles years later. "But people whose respect means the most to me didn't believe it," she added. "That helped me a lot."

For anyone dealing with the loss of a job or a business, a personal challenge such as a health crisis or, as in Dunn's case, both, support is crucial. Supporters or allies are the ones who offer a listening ear, as well as the perspective that there is a way forward. It will be up to the individual to make his or her own way by strategizing, devising ideas, and exploring possibilities, but it may very well be a friend or supporter who helps open the door to whatever comes next.

When the ordeal was over, Dunn could have exited the public spotlight. Instead, she granted a media interview about what she endured, perhaps as a way of acknowledging those who had stood by her and provided unquestioning support. In the *Fortune* magazine article published in May 2007, Dunn explained her decision to speak out about the experience. "At one level, I don't care what people who don't know me think about me. But I also have to think about my legacy. The idea that my grandchildren can Google me ten years from now and see horrible information that goes to the heart of my character distresses me. I need to do what I can do to change that."[12]

Part of Dunn's legacy is the accomplishments she's achieved since her corporate life ended. Instead of retreating, Dunn has applied her expertise, knowledge, and leadership by serving on boards of several nonprofit organizations, including UCSF Medical Center, the San Francisco Symphony, and Larkin Street Youth Services. "They have become super important to me, and the work they do is extremely worthwhile," Dunn said. "I'm as busy as I could want to be, and working with people who are active in business at very senior levels but who make the time to help these organizations succeed."

Despite all she's gone through, from the Hewlett-Packard scandal to her continued battle against cancer, Dunn has maintained a hopeful outlook, based on feeling good each day—a grateful contrast with days of setbacks. "If I felt bad I couldn't be hopeful. I've had many times in the past five years—95 percent of the time—when I felt really good. Feeling bad was usually related to having surgery and recovering," Dunn explained. "Having gotten back on track after a setback makes me feel even better; knowing I could hit a low physically and think that I may never get back. And then I did. Just be totally candid about it, if you feel good you can be optimistic."

Dunn also observed that even the toughest adversity can bring some blessings. "I think good can come out of these things," she said. "I can say that if you have a foundation these situations can turn out to be a tremendous strengthening. It's the kind of thing that helps you get your priorities straight if they aren't already— very, very quickly."

Dunn serves as a role model of the liberation that comes from admitting the truth of how difficult and challenging things are, even when the outlook is bleak and the consequences dire. From there, possibilities can be considered and battles waged. But first, there must be a reckoning to assess what has changed forever and what remains. For Dunn, this led to the affirmation of her priorities, from health to her family. Her life may have become very different from the CEO world she once occupied. But from where she sits, the lesson is clearly that "life goes on."

My advice is you have to gut it out. Go through the pain. You'd like to change things, but you can't.

—CHRIS GALVIN,
FORMER THIRD-GENERATION
CEO OF MOTOROLA INC.

Chapter Four

CHRISTOPHER GALVIN
THE POWER OF RESILIENCE

C hristopher Galvin, former third-generation CEO of Motorola Inc., believes in the power of resilience. In a conversation about his long-time career at the company founded by his grandfather, he described how every generation of his family had to rely on the ability to rebound as they built Motorola into a global technology and telecommunications company. "We are a pretty resilient lot," he reflected. "The reason Motorola worked when the Galvins ran it is that we're a highly resilient people."

In fact, one could say that the power to come back from setback or adversity has been the family's legacy, just as much as the company that for generations was synonymous with the Galvin name. Listening to Galvin tell the story of the founding of Motorola by his grandfather, Paul, the theme of resilience and embracing timeless principles were laced throughout.

Paul Galvin had a lifelong passion to run his own business, but twice his dreams ended in bankruptcy in the 1920s. First, he was betrayed by his CFO who failed to pay the company's taxes and absconded with the cash. The second time, he was beset by his own lack of imagination; entering into businesses where he was a copycat trying to compete on efficiency and price. An honorable man, after his second bankruptcy, Paul worked for Brach's, the candy company, for a while to repay all of his early investors.

Undeterred by his track record thus far, in 1928 Paul and his brother Joe started a third company, originally named Galvin

Manufacturing Corporation, having purchased from one of his defunct companies a patent for an innovation called the "battery eliminator" for home radios. When the stock market crashed, however, demand for the battery eliminator dried up, and Paul needed yet another new idea for his business to survive. Then Paul saw an opportunity that would launch him in a new market. He broke away from the crowd of home radio manufacturers and began installing radios in automobiles. When Paul's innovation caught on, he came up with a brand name for it: Motorola, to connote music on wheels, combining motor car and the Victrola phonograph. Later it also became the corporation's name.

"Paul's failures in his early days provided him with tenets that became the underpinnings of success for him and his company: surround yourself with the highest principled and most talented people; consider every employee to be the company's most important asset; resist entering a 'today's business,' but instead chase the doable, yet provable new business," remarked Galvin, who seventy years after his grandfather started the company took his turn as CEO of Motorola. "For Paul, the future was the safest place to be. If you could do market research on the new business, then often it was too late. As an innovator and entrepreneur, Paul turned his fortunes around by adhering to the highest principles and continuously seeking the next new business to enter."

From Paul Galvin's automobile radios, Motorola ventured into two-way police radios and military walkie-talkies in the 1930s, followed in the late 1940s and 1950s by television, semiconductors, and radio paging. Later, a Motorola radio was installed on the first lunar rover, launching the company in the space business that would culminate with the Iridium space-based satellite communication project, which was a technological and global project management triumph, although a major and embarrassing commercial defeat. The company also championed cellular telephony, and along the way developed the Six Sigma quality improvement process that has since become widely adopted by manufacturing companies around the world.

The theme of going against the grain runs deep in the family's story. "Every time the Galvins backed something really new, many experts of the day said it won't work," Galvin said. He took particular pride in giving examples of early Motorola products that proved the naysayers wrong: In the late 1930s, Paul Gavin went to the Pentagon to demonstrate how a portable backpack two-way radio worked but, ultimately, was turned down. Military communications experts at the time told Paul that "radios like these will never be used by the military," Galvin recounted. The Secret Service, however, bought six two-way radios to help bolster security for President Franklin D. Roosevelt. Noticing agents carrying around backpacks to tote tall transmission poles, FDR asked what they were doing. "Protecting you, Mr. President," they replied. As Galvin's story goes, Roosevelt told them, "If those radios are good enough to protect me, why aren't they good enough to protect our infantry?" With that, Motorola established the military portable radio business, which took off for the company.

Galvin also spoke of his father, Bob, who was named CEO in 1959 and remained Motorola's senior-most executive until 1990. Bob backed his team of innovators to build a mobile cellular demonstration in Washington, D.C., in the summer of 1971—a decade before the industry began. Bob resisted the skeptics who asked who could afford to pay two, four, or even six times the cost of a home telephone call to use a mobile device. Bob paid no heed and ratcheted up Motorola's R&D investments in cellular phone technology in the 1970s—even though a forty-country market research study in 1978 predicted that the total number of cellular subscribers would grow only to 900,000 by the year 2000. Bob Galvin's foresight paid off: by 2000, the cellular industry was selling about 900,000 phones globally every nineteen hours.

Chris Galvin continued the legacy. In the mid-1990s, communications experts scoffed at his prediction that wire-line phone calls would some day be made over TV cable networks, believing that those networks could never be upgraded enough to match the quality of the Bell Telephone system and provide competitive service. Like the two generations before him, Galvin stood up against conventional thinking and gave support to building a business around Motorola's invention of the cable modem in the late 1980s, thus founding a new communications segment: cable telephony and data broadband in the 1990s. (Galvin noted with a smile that wire-line phone service, which was considered "impossible" in the mid-1990s, is used today at his summer home.)

"Being an innovator or backing innovators is a lonely thing. You have to stand up when no one believes you," Galvin said, adding that senior leadership must have the resolve to do at least three things: First, be willing to take the criticism when others doubt; second, protect teams of innovators and give them time to produce results; and, third, do everything in one's power to continue providing resources and investment to innovators. "Believe me, the Galvins were not perfect by any stretch, but there is example after example of trying, failing, being criticized, learning, trying again, and eventually discovering a few really big wins. The Galvins' strategy for Motorola, simply stated, was 'continuous renewal.' "

Recounting his leadership at Motorola, Galvin rarely used the word "I" and spoke mostly in terms of "we"—usually when referring to himself and his father, along with company employees whom he called "Motorolans." No matter that Motorola grew to become a $30 billion publicly traded company, to the Galvins it was first and foremost a family firm.

For Chris Galvin, it was also a large part of his identity and where he spent virtually his entire professional career. While a student at Northwestern University, where he received a bachelor's of science degree in political science and then an MBA with distinction at the Kellogg School of Management, Galvin held part-time summer assignments at Motorola. After graduating, he took on full-time sales, sales management, and marketing management positions at the company. From there he became marketing manager and then general manager of the semiconductor equipment unit; vice president and director of the radio paging division; corporate vice president and general manager of paging; and then chief corporate staff officer and later senior vice president of the corporation. In 1990, he was promoted to the post of assistant chief operating officer and the third member of the office of the CEO. He was named president and chief operating officer in 1993, followed by CEO in 1997, and chairman and CEO in 1999.

It must have been a particularly proud moment for Galvin to take charge of the company, following in the footsteps of his father and grandfather. Expectations for his leadership ran high right from the start. A *New York Times* article in November of 1996, announcing Galvin would become CEO the following January 1, noted that his "ascension to the top of the company . . . had long been seen as all but inevitable . . . " Although the company stated at the time that the management changes reflected succession plans, the article cited analysts' speculation that the board had been unhappy with a sharp drop in earnings after several years of unusually rapid growth.[1] It would be up to Galvin to restore the growth of the company.

Things would not go as Galvin planned, however. Even though he would stake his claim to the company's eventual turnaround, Galvin found himself needing to go back to the drawing board in 1998 and 2000—not unlike his grandfather before founding Motorola in the late 1920s. Fortunately for Galvin, he had resilience on his side.

Facing the Business Battles

As the new CEO of Motorola, Galvin had a goal, which he had set with his father, of transforming Motorola so it could burst through the $30 billion revenue level and then eventually grow profitably past $100 billion. An empirical study had showed that companies

typically hit the wall in size and/or complexity and grind to a halt
(or worse) at regular sales intervals. Paul Galvin had taken the
company from $10 million to $250 million in sales. Bob grew it
from $2 billion in revenues to $10 billion, and put in place the
cellular business and operations in China to grow to $25 billion by
the mid-1990s. It would be up to Chris to tackle the next targets.

"You can't decide what happens when you show up," Galvin
said stoically. Six months after he took over as CEO in 1997—as he
and Bob Gowney, who was chief operating officer (COO) at the
time, successfully executed on an efficiency drive to save $750
million in order to improve earnings by another $400 million and
allocate an additional $350 million to R&D—the Asian currency
crisis hit. With its large operations in China and other parts of Asia,
Motorola went from a 1998 plan to make $2 billion in operating
earnings to losing $1 billion in sixty days in late 1997. Then in 2001
came the dot-com bust, September 11, the semiconductor recession, and other challenges.

These events added topspin to the overall pattern of volatility
that was to be expected for a company in the business of launching
new ventures. "If your goal over the next quarter century is to
invent new industries, it's difficult to predict precisely the cycle
time to invention and/or the acceptance of that invention," Galvin
said. "It takes at least a decade to create a new multi-billion-dollar
global industry segment. If the industry is new, there is no history to
study in order to determine when customers would start to purchase, for example, a microprocessor–motion sensor combination
control to turn on a water faucet by waving your hand, instead of
purchasing a faucet handle. Therefore, less-than-smooth quarterly
earnings were the occasional, but conscious, investment trade-off."

Galvin faced other challenges such as Motorola's $5 billion
Iridium satellite phone system that went online in 1998 and
performed to its original technical specifications set in the early
1990s but realized a very low customer usage rate. Iridium resulted in a $740 million charge taken in 1998 and a $3.5 billion

bondholder lawsuit in 2002.[2] "No question, it did not work commercially," Galvin said of Iridium. "We lost $2 billion or so on it and transferred it to companies serving the U.S. government, which has since put it to good use."

On Iridium, Galvin shared a story he said was never made public before, of a conversation that he had with his father in late 1999, at a time when the press was being negative on Iridium and, as a result, the younger Galvin's leadership. "Dad said, 'Chris, blame Iridium on me. After all, I made the call. Get it off your plate,'" Galvin recalled. He thanked his father for the selfless offer but refused to allow him to take the bullet.

"First off, for me to allow my father to take the fall for Iridium would have been disingenuous. I voted in favor of doing Iridium as did all of the Motorola directors on every board vote over a decade," he added. "Second and much more important, laying blame on any one person for failed innovation might have poisoned our culture of high innovation at Motorola. On my watch as CEO I did not want to send any message, subtle or direct, to any of our innovators other than, 'If you fail in legitimate efforts to create new opportunities and you learn from it (i.e., not repeat the mistake again), you are worth more—not less. We just invested in your education. Keep innovating. We win and lose as a team.'"

By 2003, the company appeared to be making headway, with a profit reported for the first quarter and a prediction that it would stay profitable through the 2003 fiscal year. The Motorola letter to shareholders in the 2002 annual report, published in 2003, pledged: "We expect to grow the way we did prior to the artificially inflated growth that resulted from the telecom and dot-com booms in the late 1990s and the period of decline that followed in 2001 and 2002: steadily, rationally, with real products serving real needs in real marketplaces." Markets in which Motorola was already established, Motorola management predicted, would "return to solid, steady growth."

The shareholders letter, signed by Galvin and then–Motorola president and COO Mike Zafirovski, also promised growth of approximately 3 percent in 2003. "Beyond this we anticipate growth rates to improve as the world stabilizes and our strategies take hold."[3]

The positive uptrend in the company's fortunes were aided significantly in 2001–2003 by tough decisions made by Galvin and his team in response to global and economic challenges faced by Motorola. "I made the mistake of allowing too much manufacturing, engineering, and marketing capacity to be added during the late 1990s dot-com boom and then had to remove it," Galvin said. As CEO, Galvin made a total of $12 billion in write-offs, laid off 55,000 out of 150,000 employees, closed 42 percent of facilities worldwide, hired prolifically from the outside, adopted General Electric's leadership supply system, reinvented Six Sigma by digitizing it, and changed out seventy of one hundred top leaders over eighteen months—all while investing heavily in research and development.

Given the scope of Motorola's operations—four of its six business groups were large enough to be multi-billion-dollar Fortune 500 businesses on their own—a turnaround of the company was a massive task. Unfortunately, a situation beyond anyone's control would hit Motorola's results, despite the promise for growth in 2003. The cause this time was the spread of severe acute respiratory syndrome (SARS) through China. Motorola, which ranked as one of China's largest U.S. companies at the time with 12,000 workers, had to shut its main office after an employee there came down with SARS. Similarly, it closed down a production line in Singapore due to a SARS case. In June 2003, Motorola announced lower expectations for revenues in the second quarter and the full year due to the impact of SARS, as Asian consumers stopped going to malls to shop for cell phones for nearly two months in the spring of 2003 because of fear of SARS, which could be fatal.

Meanwhile, the Motorola board of directors grew impatient when the result of Galvin's actions in 2001–2003 produced improvement but not strong turnaround financial results as yet. In September 2003, two company directors met Galvin in his office to deliver a board decision that completely blindsided him: They wanted Galvin to step down.

Galvin tried to reason with board members, telling them that the turnaround plan was completed and results would soon materialize. He asked them to reconsider the decision over the upcoming weekend; to continue discussions and set milestones going forward. Galvin also reminded the two directors that they had both promised him personally that there would be no surprises in matters of CEO succession. But the directors' minds were made up. As they saw it, once they started the process of asking him to leave and recruiting his replacement, they couldn't stop. Owning 3 percent of the outstanding Motorola shares, the Galvin family did not control enough of the stock to block the board's decision.

Galvin had no choice but to agree to leave and, in that meeting, offered the two directors a prediction regarding his successor, no matter who it turned out to be. "I told them, 'If you take me out, no matter who you pick as CEO, he or she will be on the cover of every major business magazine in 2004–2005 for the Motorola Inc. turnaround I have already led.'"

When the board members left his office and Galvin emerged, his secretary observed that "he looked like he died." Grim-faced as he told the story, Galvin added, "I'm sure I did." First he called his wife, Cindy, to let her know what had happened and to figure out how to tell their two sons. Then he called his father. The elder Galvin's response was supportive, acknowledging the challenges that his son had faced, including a board composed of decent people but with "too many average thinkers."

By far the most emotionally draining experience of this setback, Galvin recalled, was dealing with the reaction of his team, which ranged from shock to anger to disbelief. "Men, some of my direct reports, cried in my office, and I was trying to calm them down. The reaction was that they were appalled. They kept saying over and over, 'This is impossible. Look at the positive cash flow and operating earnings progress. Why now? Why this way?'"

If there was any consolation for Galvin, it might have been the parting shot he fired in the announcement of his pending "retirement" from Motorola. Normally when a company announces that the CEO is stepping down, the wording downplays any disagreements and presents a unified front that somehow the action being taken is for the best of all involved. Instead, the statement regarding Galvin's departure included a tersely worded quote from him: "The board and I do not share the same view of the company's pace, strategy and progress."

Looking back, Galvin underscored the intention of that comment: "I wanted to be very clear publicly in September 2003. I disagreed with the board's assessment that poor Motorola financial performance would be forthcoming because of my leadership as CEO."

For the coming months, Galvin dealt with the numbing reality that his thirty-six years at Motorola, starting when he was sixteen years old, were over. Even more of a blow was watching his prophecy of record-setting financial performance at Motorola come true, which became the proverbial salt in the wound. He was forced out of the company just as the turnaround was coming to fruition.

A Lame Duck CEO

In the days immediately following the board's decision, Galvin found himself in circumstances that must have felt surreal at the time. He offered to stay on and run the company until a new CEO was hired—in effect becoming the "lame duck CEO." The week after his departure announcement was made, Motorola was staging the seventy-fifth anniversary of the founding of the company with a celebration that was to be held in the Galvin Center, a museum commemorating the milestones in the company's—and his family's—history. Chris and Bob Galvin, along with company president and COO Mike Zafirovski, presided over the event, which the board did not attend. "We did our very best to rally the troops and thank employees for their dedication and contribution, while we figuratively stood over our open caskets at a funeral-wake for Bob and Chris Galvin in Motorola's future," Galvin said.

Like so many CEOs in similar circumstances, after the announcement that he was stepping down was released, Galvin saw his performance as a top executive dissected in the media. *The New York Times*, for example, described his six years as CEO as "tumultuous" and noted the "increasing frustration Motorola board members had with his performance."[4]

These reports on his supposedly poor performance must have had Galvin tearing out his hair, knowing that soon-to-be released numbers would show his efforts to turn around the company were paying off. Just two weeks after the board's announcement, Motorola began four rolling quarters (October 2003 through September 2004) of growth, with sales revenue up 27 percent and earnings improving by 187 percent. Motorola also announced that new bookings for new customer orders in its $12 billion handset business (mobile phones) were 44 percent ahead of the prior year, and total company bookings were up 25 percent from the year-ago period.

Motorola's prospects were even brighter for the fourth-quarter of 2003, when Galvin was still CEO, with a 64 percent increase in bookings in handsets compared with a year earlier. Across all six of its business sectors, overall new product bookings gained 42 percent. Quarter after quarter of record-setting financial results and the free cash flow that was generated would eventually earn Galvin's turnaround of Motorola acclaim as one of the top five accomplished since 1990 among high-technology companies with more than $5 billion in revenues, according to a study conducted by the Monitor Group. Motorola's results made the list along with firms such as IBM (1992–1997), Hewlett-Packard (2003–2007), Apple (1996–2001), and Xerox (2000–2005).

From September 2003 until his departure in January 2004, Galvin busied himself with running the business and supporting

Zafirovski. The day that Galvin left Motorola, the firm was the "fastest growing company in the Fortune 60," he said—no small feat for a $30 billion firm.

Although Galvin's role in Motorola's turnaround was never publicly acknowledged by the company, he said one director later expressed regret and another wrote to him. Those gestures, however, didn't change the fact that Galvin had to leave the company founded by his grandfather.

Galvin's successor was Ed Zander, former president of Sun Microsystems, who was described in the media as "a highly regarded outsider from Silicon Valley." As the new CEO at Motorola, Zander acknowledged in a *New York Times* article the work that had already been done to rebuild the company's balance sheet and return to profitability, and said Motorola was in need of a "turn up" not a turnaround.[5]

The Worst Six Months of His Life

Galvin departed Motorola, although he was notionally a consultant to the company. Then came the real blow: watching Motorola post even better results with its stellar performance for the first quarter of 2004—numbers that if they had arrived a few quarters sooner would have been Galvin's to announce as the sitting CEO. In the first-quarter of 2004, Motorola showed a 42 percent rise in sales growth. It posted an approximately 10 percent operating margin, added over $800 million in free cash, and, for the first time in its history, had a balance sheet with more cash than debt. But the CEO in charge when those results were announced was Zander, not Galvin. And as Galvin had predicted to the board, it was his successor whose name was associated with the results.

Then in the third quarter of 2004, Motorola introduced the RAZR, a trendy cellular phone that was hailed in the media as a runaway success with a record 100 million of the phones sold— setting all-time sales volume records in its price category at the time. RAZR was unveiled on Zander's watch, although the phone's development was completed in the fourth quarter of 2003, when Galvin was still leading the company.

During this time, Galvin was on the sidelines enduring a painful transition period—particularly the six months following his departure from the CEO suite, when he purposefully didn't even contemplate what might come next. That advice had come from Jamie Dimon, who as president of Citigroup had been fired by his longtime boss Sandy Weill. On a Saturday morning in September 2003, about twelve hours after Galvin's departure was announced by the board, Dimon called Galvin at home. "He said, 'Chris, I've been through this before. It was awful. You have to promise me one thing. When you step out the door, you won't do one thing for six months. I don't care if the next Google calls you,'" Galvin recalled.

Other calls of support had come in from Henry "Hank" Paulson, then CEO of Goldman Sachs, which was Motorola's investment banker, and from McKinsey & Company partners who had worked closely with the company. "I'll never forget what they did for me," Galvin said.

For Galvin, the waiting period that Dimon advised didn't start until January 2004, when the new CEO was in place. At that point, Galvin dealt with the reality of life after Motorola. Although many CEOs endure difficult transitions—being asked to step down or retiring sooner than they would have planned—for Galvin the pain must have been double. This was no ordinary company; this was the firm founded by his grandfather—his family legacy. For the first time in seventy-five years, the Galvins were out of Motorola.

Galvin's six-month self-imposed hiatus forced him to live in the present instead of planning for the future as he had done all his life. "Not being in forward motion made it the worst six months of my life, but I highly respected Jamie Dimon's advice; he had been through it before. I knew I had to listen to him," he said. "It was hard when my real life's passion was Motorola."

Finally, the six months were over. Sitting on the front porch at his father's house, Galvin received unwavering support for his successful turnaround at Motorola and some valuable advice. "Dad said, 'I'm not going to let those people [Motorola board members] ruin the rest of my life, nor should you.'" Galvin recalled that he thought about it for a minute and then said, "'Dad, you're right. Let's start over.'"

With that, Chris and Bob Galvin began to plan for what would come next.

Starting Over

The first order of business was to extricate the Galvin family money from Motorola shares. Galvin set a goal to sell all the family's Motorola stock within three years of the date of the board's announcement of his departure. Over the next two-and-a-half years, the Galvin family exited more than 99.5 percent of its zero tax-basis shares. The next step was to figure out how to apply not only their capital, but also their experience and network of contacts to a new venture in a way that would enable them to "stay in the business of transforming industry" and "hang with the world's best investors," as Galvin described.

Galvin explained that at Motorola, he and his father had run one of "the world's largest venture capital companies," incubating businesses and even entire industries. That was a legacy the Galvins wanted to continue in their next venture, albeit on a smaller scale. Little surprise, then, that Galvin has a big vision behind his new businesses. Sitting in the conference room in the offices of Harrison Street Capital, LLC in downtown Chicago, Galvin laid out the new ventures he's launched, which have grown from one employee (Galvin) to more than 600 over the past four years.

One of them, Harrison Street Capital, is a private-equity fund founded by Galvin, his father, and his brother, Michael. Another, Harrison Street Real Estate Capital LLC, cofounded with

Christopher Merrill in 2005, is a real estate private equity firm with approximately $1.8 billion in real estate assets that it owns or has under development. Harrison Street Real Estate focuses on "recession-resistant assets," with a portfolio of properties such as student housing, senior housing and assisted living units, self-storage, marina berths, and rentable medical office space. "We seek to innovate in everything," Galvin said. "We are the first to apply Six Sigma Quality to the design of a real estate private equity business model."

Although the name "Galvin" isn't on any of these businesses, the family legacy is still there. Harrison Street is where Paul Galvin and his brother Joe established Galvin Manufacturing Company, his third but first successful company, which later became Motorola. "We took inspiration from Paul's example to start over," Galvin said.

Among the more interesting ventures is The Galvin Projects, a virtual global think tank led by Bob Galvin, which has taken on such problems as efficient electrical grids and relieving urban traffic congestion. The elder Galvin's vision is to create one million permanent jobs in the United States that can't be exported to Asia. What better place to start than the power industry, combining the principles of Six Sigma, reliability methodologies developed by Bell Labs, and the top people from the Electric Power Research Institute, an independent nonprofit research, development, and design company in the electricity sector. One of the first projects studied was something Galvin called "intelligent micro-grids" to improve power supply and distribution, as explained in the book, *Perfect Power: How the Microgrid Revolution Will Unleash Cleaner, Greener, More Abundant Energy*, co-authored by his father and published in 2008.

Rounding out the new ventures is Gore Creek Asset Management, LLC, a large-capital investment company. "In redeploying the bulk of our capital we decided to build our own global investment business," Galvin said. "Emulating the business model of the Harvard and Yale endowments, we wanted direct contact with the global investment managers doing the investing. They became part of our new global business intelligence system, and I became part of theirs."

The ventures are varied and, especially in the case of the Galvin Projects, forward-looking into possibilities not yet realized. As Galvin described giving support to new digital storage methods, the prospect of inventing new ways to write software, and doing roll-ups in defense services and more, his excitement was palpable. Although his current suite of offices is dwarfed in comparison with the sprawling corporate complex of Motorola and its global operations, Galvin's eyes are clearly on the future. "The Galvins define leadership as taking people elsewhere—to a place that people would never go unless you, the leader, were there," he reflected.

In order to move forward with these new ventures, Galvin needed to own the turnaround he orchestrated at Motorola. This may represent some unfinished business for him, but is equally important to illustrate his leadership and management success to potential investors in his new companies. This is a lesson for anyone who is getting back on track after a job loss or other career upset: past accomplishments must be recognized in order to find the confidence to begin again. Galvin calls this process "rebooting," starting up again just like a computer that has been shut down. And just like with a computer, a successful personal reboot requires a solid operating system. For individuals, this means having an authentic and realistic view of themselves, admitting one's mistakes, and claiming accomplishments.

"When you reboot, you have to find out who you really are. When you step away from the platform [of a previous job, position, or title]—the minute that goes away—you look at yourself in the mirror and see what you have accomplished. Those who can't reboot don't have the confidence to do it again," Galvin observed.

From media interviews to speeches on corporate governance, Galvin has used the numbers to make his case that his role in the turnaround of Motorola was critical. "The work we did in 2000, up to 2003, turned out to pay off in 2004, 2005, and 2006," Galvin told the *Chicago Tribune*. "And then the decisions that were made by subsequent leaders in the business in 2004, 2005, and 2006 delivered to the shareholders the results of 2007."[6] The losses that Motorola experienced in 2007 then continued in 2008 and into 2009.

After posting solid earnings in 2004, 2005, and 2006, Motorola began struggling again, losing ground in market share and cutting prices that hurt margins. "As a result, Motorola, which had long had the second largest share of the market behind Nokia, fell to third place behind Samsung Electronics, and its profits have suffered," the *New York Times* wrote.[7] In November 2007, Motorola announced Zander was retiring and was stepping down as CEO.

Although the numbers appeared to vindicate his leadership at Motorola, Galvin's only option was to move on.

The Importance of Resilience

Sitting in his office at Harrison Street Capital, Galvin continued to digest all that has happened since his departure from Motorola, including the lessons learned. Not surprisingly, many of the lessons had to do with resilience.

Resilience is a necessary characteristic in leadership, enabling someone not only to persevere in the midst of difficulty or hardship, but also to learn important lessons and grow as a result of it. In an interview, Diane Coutu, retired senior editor of *Harvard Business Review*, explained that an individual's level of resilience has a big influence on the choices taken after an upset such as the loss of a job or the failure of a business. In fact, overcoming hardship and resilience are two factors that can elevate leadership.

"In America we are in deep denial about the importance of obstacles. We don't want our leaders to have any flaws or obstacles in their journey," Coutu explained.

However, heroes from life and literature are often those who have had to face significant challenges. Coutu cited Franklin Roosevelt, who overcame the limitations of paralysis, and Teddy Roosevelt, who battled depression, as did Abraham Lincoln. "Very many people do not learn lessons while they are in power, but when they have been brought down," Coutu said. "Generally resilience is harder to learn on the job."

For Galvin, being asked to step down from the CEO post just as the turnaround he had promised was beginning to show results provided several lessons. Among those lessons was the acknowledgment that, despite one's plans and best intentions, outside forces cannot be changed and controlled. On a more personal level for Galvin, he also learned not to put himself or his next venture again in a position where others who don't understand or share his vision can override his plans. "What's the learning for me? The only protection, as Paul learned in one of his bankruptcies, is to surround oneself with partners, directors, executives, and employees whom the leader believes can be trusted with good judgment," he said.

Galvin's observation may ring true for many entrepreneurs who come out of the corporate world where they felt their plans were thwarted and projects were misunderstood or derailed or both. In order to stay true to their vision, they launch businesses of their own, without relinquishing decision making or the need to seek others' approval.

Another resilience factor Coutu stressed was the importance of values—not in being good or bad, but rather having a resolve that is based on what is most important to that individual. One of Galvin's values since his departure from Motorola has been better corporate governance, a campaign he has taken public, such as with a May 2008 presentation at a conference at Northwestern University's Kellogg School of Management to address the issue of short-term market pressure on boards and management.

On board governance, Galvin draws from his own experience as a director of NAVTEQ, a technology spin-off company. He helped form the independent board of directors that took NAVTEQ public during the summer of 2004 at $22 a share and became the chairman. The share price ran up to $55 and then collapsed to $23 after the company missed earnings estimates by a penny. Keeping a long-term view, NAVTEQ's board stayed true to its vision. In October 2007, the company was sold to Nokia for $78 a share—a 255 percent return from the July 2004 IPO to the final close of the deal in 2008. By contrast, over the same four-year period, Motorola's share price declined nearly 60 percent.

A correlating lesson for Galvin is the importance of managing the expectations of others—including board members, shareholders, and analysts—and of emphasizing the long-term, instead of succumbing to Wall Street's predilection for quarterly results above all. Galvin sees a danger in having a short-term focus, which can undermine innovation and competitiveness.

"It's not hard for us to stand up to people," Galvin said, referring to himself, his father, and his grandfather. "It's a belief system that says innovation—introducing the new—is doable and repeatable every decade. It's a matter of survival."

A third characteristic of resilience is improvisation, which Coutu defined as "the ability to come up with new solutions . . . to improve constantly and continuously." From the early days of Motorola to the latest ventures, Galvin and his family have demonstrated the ability to improvise and innovate, turning ideas into business opportunities. As Galvin observed, "The most terrifying thing to look at is a blank piece of paper—not because there is nothing to do, but because we have so many things we can do."

Another trait of resilience is mastery, specifically of whatever challenge or circumstance is confronting a person. "Mastery is a very psychological word. Let's look at someone with posttraumatic stress disorder. You don't get over PTSD, but people can learn to master that anxiety, to live with it in the real world," Coutu explained. Even when a person cannot get over all that has happened in the midst of a personal or professional upheaval—some unresolved issues from the past might always remain—mastery puts the individual in control."

For Galvin, the challenge he has had to master is to put Motorola behind him while taking the credit for the turnaround that began to surface soon after his departure. "We are proud of our work at Motorola," Galvin said. "It was a great run." Although his family name will always be associated with Motorola, increasingly Galvin is showing his mastery as his energy turns to the future instead of the past.

"Gut It Out" and Other Lessons Learned

The final quality that characterizes resilience according to Coutu is the ability to attract supporters. To illustrate, Coutu used the example of a person who is seriously ill and needs to engage the support of caretakers. "You have got to give to the other person before they can give to you. To be that survivor, you have to take the first step. To me, that's paradoxical, but those who understand that are very much more resilient," she explained. "Resilience is interactive." The same could be said for those going through upheaval in their professional lives who seek out others to help and champion them.

Galvin, however, sees it somewhat differently. Although having supporters—especially his wife, father, mother, brother, and lawyer—was meaningful, nothing could replace or circumvent the need to go through the emotional turmoil of leaving Motorola himself. He found value in going it alone and facing the pain of the transition process head-on. "You have to process it yourself. Nobody can talk you out of what you are feeling. People say all kinds of nice things, but that doesn't take away the pain," Galvin said. "There wasn't anybody who could do that. It's just time."

Galvin's observation led to an emotion-packed lesson learned that can be applied equally in life or business: "My advice is you just have to gut it out. Go through the pain," he explained. "You'd like to change it, but you can't."

Summing up his lessons learned Galvin turned philosophical as he considered what he had gained from the entire experience:

"People are the most important asset. They can be your biggest joy or your biggest disappointment."

Galvin returned again to the family history: He told a tragic story involving his grandmother, Lillian, who was murdered in her home. At the time, Bob Galvin had left Notre Dame to join the war effort. Early one evening, coming home from Northwestern University where he was being trained in the signal corps, Bob found his mother and the maid shot dead in a day-time burglary. Unable to reach his father, Paul, who was on a train coming home from New York, Bob had to go to the station to tell him the horrible news.

"Paul went bankrupt twice and tragically lost Lillian, his wife. Dad lost his mother tragically and, in his retirement, he watched the Motorola board unravel his fifty-five-year investment in the company's culture. I suffered little in comparison with my grandfather and father, but I did lose one thing that was dear to me: the opportunity to create innovation and contribute to the world in partnership with a great team at Motorola," Galvin reflected.

Although the family's legacy has been to overcome setbacks and tragedies, an important part of the story has also been to build for the future. Galvin has his sights on what Harrison Street Capital might mean for the next generation, possibly including his two sons: one a double major in physics and economics who is now in graduate school at Kellogg School of Management, and the other a physics major who graduated cum laude from Harvard. "There's some real talent," Galvin said with a broad smile.

No doubt thinking of how Galvin Manufacturing became Motorola, Galvin sees similar potential for Harrison Street Capital one day. "I'm building it up for my sons, their cousins, and their kids, and the many very talented non-family professionals who will join us," he said. "This is for the next generation to lead: numerous and hopefully big businesses, a new brand with global capacity to influence. I can help teach them to do that, and then they can make the world a better place. Paul Galvin dreamed big. Eighty years later, we can, too."

You learn it's not about you at all. . . .
There's nothing you can do. You have to
accept that it's not about you at all.

Chapter Five

HERBERT "PUG" WINOKUR
AFTER THE STORM

I n the corporate world, "Enron" packs the punch of a four-letter word. Since the company's bankruptcy filing in late 2001, its name and crooked E logo have become synonymous with management fraud, an inflated stock that dissolved into worthlessness, and top executives who went to jail. Employees who held stock options or shares in the company lost not only their jobs, but also their pensions and their life savings.

In the public mind, including much of the media, Enron was so toxic that even a remote association was enough to stain someone's reputation. For Herbert "Pug" Winokur, some fifteen years of service on the Enron board put him in the spotlight as the media, lawmakers, and investors tried to fathom what had happened and who was to blame. Even when he volunteered to serve on a special investigative committee of the Enron board that was tasked with figuring out what had caused the demise of the company, Winokur faced criticism—including from Congress—as to whether he, a long-term board member, should serve on that panel.

When Winokur first became a board member of Enron back in the mid-1980s, the company then was called Houston Natural Gas and was in the natural gas pipeline business. Over the years, the company morphed from operating only gas pipelines at first into trading and a variety of operations from international energy projects to a broadband venture. In the process, Enron became the darling of investors and Wall Street analysts—a New Economy firm that through the late 1990s and into the early 2000s boasted big ideas and a portfolio of global assets. As *Newsweek* noted: "Unlike flaky Internet start-ups that substituted ethereal yardsticks like 'eyeballs' and 'stickiness' for revenues and profits, Enron had real businesses, real assets, real revenues and what seemed to be real profits. It owned natural gas pipelines and electricity-generating plants and water companies. Not only would it do well, it would improve the planet by substituting the efficient hand of the market for the clumsy hand of government regulation." By 2000, Enron was No. 7 on the Fortune 500. It topped lists of most admired companies and best places to work. "The guys running the show were hailed as magicians with newfound secrets that would change the future of business," *Newsweek* added.[1]

In time, however, Enron's growth and prosperity became more illusion than fact when company management crossed the line from running a legitimate business and began to engage in improper off-balance-sheet transactions to obfuscate Enron's financial condition. When Enron unraveled into a massive and complex bankruptcy in late 2001, it became a symbol of corporate excess, greed, and questionable activities in pursuit of an ever-higher stock price.

When fingers were pointed as to who was responsible and who should have known about the apparent management misdeeds that resulted in criminal charges filed against some top executives, members of the board became an easy and understandable target. The lingering question asked openly and repeatedly by the press and other observers was, "What did the board know?"

For Winokur, Enron became a crucible as he and other Enron board members faced intense scrutiny. In the midst of the turmoil, he had to contend with the clouds of doubt and suspicion, which cast a wide shadow on anyone associated with the company.

In the end, his consolation and vindication has come from the fact that, as visible and public as he was during the six years that followed Enron's demise—during bankruptcy proceedings and at hearings before Congress, the Securities and Exchange

Commission (SEC), the Justice Department, creditor committees, numerous private lawsuits, and the Department of Labor—neither his fellow outside directors nor he were ever charged with any wrongdoing. Through the ordeal, rather than focusing only on the hearings and the testimony, he pursued a quest of his own: to find out what had happened at Enron. The board's special committee, on which Winokur served, produced a 200-page report on the causes of Enron's collapse. For Winokur this was a personal mission as well, allowing him to put to rest the questions in his own mind as to what had gone so wrong at the Houston-based energy, commodity, and trading company.

Connections and Opportunities

Before he became a member of the Enron board, Pug Winokur was well known as an investor with an impressive career in corporate turnarounds. His experiences in government, including working at the Pentagon and later as a consultant to the Treasury Department, and as a turnaround expert in transportation, energy, and other industries provided valuable insight into operations, management, and investment. Along the way, he worked with a who's who of entrepreneurs and leaders in business. From the beginning, he exhibited a knack for finding new opportunities. "Focus on the doors that are opening," he said, "not the ones that are closing."

Doors opened early on for Winokur, who was born in Columbus, Georgia, in December 1943. He moved at the age of two with his mother to Philadelphia to rejoin his father, who had been stationed in India with the Army Air Corps and then returned from military service to take over the family pawnbroking business. His father later sold the business and became a management consultant to small firms. Winokur went to a Quaker boys' school, the William Penn Charter School, and then to Harvard University, where he started as a sophomore, thanks to advanced placement classes he'd taken.

After graduating from Harvard in three years in 1964 with a degree in mathematics, he applied to Harvard Business School. Although he was given a firm acceptance, Winokur was told he was too young to start right away; he had to wait a year. On the advice of his undergraduate thesis advisor, Winokur enrolled in a one-year master's program in engineering and applied physics at Harvard. At the end of that year, Winokur had a master's degree and a part-time consulting job and was living in an apartment—a much more appealing life than sweating it out in Harvard Business School and being cooped up in a dorm like so many of his friends. Weighing his options, he decided to stay the course and earned a Ph.D. in decision and control theory in 1967, before his twenty-fourth birthday.

With his formal education behind him, Winokur followed a friend, who was a year older, to the U.S. Department of Defense. From 1967 to 1970, Winokur worked for two assistant secretaries of defense (systems analysis and comptroller) as part of a small analytical group at the Pentagon that included some bright young men who would go on to make big names for themselves in business: Henry "Hank" Paulson Jr., who would become chairman and CEO of Goldman Sachs and then U.S. Treasury Secretary from July 2006 through January 2009, and Bill George, who later became CEO of medical device maker Medtronic, to name only two. "All of us really believed that the analytical work we were doing would inform good policy decisions, helping people to make judgments appropriately," Winokur recalled. "We thought government could actually make a difference."

Winokur's government work drew upon his background in mathematics and analysis, key skills that he would later employ as an investor. Among the government projects that Winokur worked on was development of a model that the Air Force used for the next twenty years to evaluate the capacity of new pilot training bases. He also participated in a cash flow study for the Pentagon, which put him in contact with another Pentagon staffer: Ken Lay, the future chairman and CEO of Enron. Winokur gained further expertise in energy while working in 1970 with a Cabinet-level study group to investigate oil import controls. The study that was produced recommended for the first time that the federal government put in place underground petroleum security storage.

By 1971, Winokur was looking for something else to do. That's when he and three friends from the Pentagon—Donald Ogilvie (who later became president of the American Bankers Association), Bruce Caputo (who later served in Congress), and Clarence "Lucky" Lester (a decorated World War II fighter pilot and Tuskegee Airman)— started a consulting firm called Inner City Fund. The group had modest beginnings in Lester's basement but a big vision to make socially useful investments while consulting to pay the bills.

Among the new company's first pieces of business was a consulting contract with the government after Treasury Secretary John Connally founded an international energy policy office within the Treasury Department. With his background in energy and experience working at the Pentagon, Winokur was contacted. The newfound partnership's name, however, proved to be a momentary stumbling block. "The contract officer told us, 'I have been in my job for a lot of years and I expect to keep my job. So if you think I'm going to give a sole source contract on international energy policy to a company called Inner City Fund. . . . Go back and change your name,'" Winokur recalled with a laugh. "Then we became ICF Inc."

In 1973, wanting to branch out from government contract work, Winokur explored a new opportunity working for Victor Palmieri, a Los Angeles– and New York–based real estate financier whose firm specialized in reorganizing and restructuring large companies. This new job gave Winokur first-hand experience in turning around companies, which would add to his growing expertise and later on made him a valuable member of corporate boards.

With his first assignment with Palmieri, Winokur became immersed in the energy business: dealing with the non-rail assets of Penn Central Railroad, among them Buckeye Pipeline, which operated primarily in the East Coast and Midwest to transport crude oil and petroleum products. John McArthur, former dean of the Harvard Business School who had been one of the trustees of Penn Central during its bankruptcy, described the work Winokur did for Buckeye as brilliant. "He figured out the competitive characteristics around every possible movement of petroleum products on the Buckeye Pipeline and, given this analysis, what Buckeye could charge for it," McArthur recalled.

By the mid-1970s, Winokur had outgrown the Buckeye job and became vice president for corporate development for Pennsylvania Company, the parent of Penn Central Railroad, headed by Palmieri. Following its Penn Central work, the Palmieri Company took over Pinehurst Inc., a 9,500-acre golf resort and hotel, at the request of Citibank and other lenders; Winokur became the CEO of that business. When Palmieri was tapped to become ambassador at large and U.S. coordinator for refugee affairs for the Carter Administration, Winokur had to figure out what to do next. Richard Ferry, the co-founder of executive recruiting firm Korn/Ferry, introduced him to David Murdock, the real estate developer and mergers and acquisitions magnate who ran Pacific Holdings Corporation, a private conglomerate of industrial businesses. Winokur was hired to head Murdock's investments in 1981. Winokur honed his deal-making expertise over the next few years. Among the more interesting deals were the merger of Iowa Beef into Occidental Petroleum, which was run by legendary businessman Armand Hammer, the subsequent purchase of Cities Service Company by Occidental, and the leveraged buyout of Cannon Mills Inc. In each case, Winokur designed and executed the deal structure.

By 1983, it was time for another move. Winokur joined the executive team at Penn Central as senior executive vice president, with responsibility for all of the operating units, a member of the office of the president, and a member of the board. At the time, Penn Central had emerged from bankruptcy and purchased businesses from fiber optics to pipelines and had tax credits that made it attractive to potential partners and suitors. Between 1983 and 1987, Penn Central's Chairman Carl Lindner and CEO Al Martinelli, who had been Winokur's boss at Buckeye Pipeline, encouraged his efforts, which included downsizing the corporate office from 400 to 75 people and then selling or spinning off most of the operating units. These efforts were well received by the market, with a significant increase in Penn Central's stock price.

As a result, it was time for Winokur to once again ask the question that surfaced frequently in his career: What's next? To answer that question he sought the advice of Charlie Munger, vice chairman of Berkshire Hathaway Corp., which is chaired by Warren Buffett. Back in the 1970s, Winokur had had a three-hour interview with Munger, which had not led to a job as Winokur had hoped, but rather to an interest in "keeping in touch." This time when Winokur went to see Munger he touted his successes and accomplishments at Penn Central. Perhaps, Winokur suggested, he could become a CEO of a company that needed someone with his expertise.

As Winokur recalled, Munger had a completely different assessment of his prospects. "'You're unemployable!' he told me," Winokur recalled. "'Everywhere you go, people lose their jobs and they sell the company.'"

Looking at all he'd done, from turnarounds to acquisitions and divestitures and a good bit of management as well, Winokur decided it was time to start his own firm. In 1987, he founded Capricorn Holdings, based in Greenwich, Conn., which specializes in investing in middle market companies in the midst of "special situations," including turnarounds, mergers, acquisitions, divestitures, and capital infusions.

The Enron Board

With his business expertise and network of connections, it's not surprising that Winokur would be sought out as a board member for a major energy company. His first directorship had been in the early 1980s at U.S. Leasing, an experience he credited as a good education into "how a quality board works." Then in about 1985, he received an unexpected call from a former Pentagon colleague: Ken Lay. Houston Natural Gas had reached out to Lay to become its new CEO. With three directors retiring from the board, Lay was asked by his board to pick new directors. Among the candidates was Winokur.

"I hadn't talked to him for five years or so," Winokur said as he recalled how straightforwardly he was approached about joining Houston Natural Gas. "Ken came out to the house in Greenwich and asked me, 'Would you come on the board?'"

Before he agreed to join the board, Winokur consulted with John Williams of natural gas firm The Williams Companies, who was then on the Penn Central board. Williams advised Winokur that the experience as a director of Houston Natural Gas would be good for him. Winokur accepted Lay's offer.

Soon thereafter, another natural gas pipeline company, Internorth, made a bid to merge with Houston Natural Gas. For Internorth it was a "poison pill" move; a transaction that would load it up with debt and make it unattractive to corporate raiders looking to take over the firm. To the Houston Natural Gas board, the cash offer to sell to Internorth was very compelling and a sweet deal for its shareholders. As a result of the transaction, the combined company became HNG Internorth. Soon after the deal closed, the Internorth board fired its CEO and turned to Lay to become its CEO; the company name eventually was changed to Enron.

As a board member for Enron, Winokur served at first on the compensation committee and later became chair of the board's finance committee. The lead director was John Duncan, one of the founders of Gulf & Western Corporation, a conglomerate that boasted diverse operations, including movie and television studios, with whom Winokur is still close. "We had a lead director in those days. The board members were terrific people. We held executive sessions [widely recognized as a corporate governance best practice, with board members engaging in discussion separately from management] ten years before other companies," Winokur said.

Enron's roots were the regulated gas pipeline business, which then became unregulated around 1990. This change in the industry landscape soon had Enron exploring new ways to do business, such as branching out into trading and what became known as the "gas bank," which bought gas from producers and sold to consumers.

"It was the most admired company at the time," Winokur reflected. "We had three pieces of business: a relatively small set of pipeline assets, a very large and growing international power business, and then we had a trading business. The goal was to build up the international stuff and sell it, and pay down debt."

The picture that was later revealed, however, shows a shadowy side of Enron's plans, including partnerships set up by then-chief financial officer Andrew Fastow that were supposed to act as a hedge against specific investments. What the board never knew, Winokur maintains, was that these partnerships were really vehicles to put millions of dollars into the pockets of a few company insiders and associates, including Fastow. At the time, based on the information and recommendations presented by Lay and others and approved by auditors and legal advisors, the partnerships appeared to be legitimate and in the best interest of the company. In time, that would prove not to be the case.

The Harvard Connection

Concurrent with his directorship at Enron, Winokur was expanding his involvement in other areas of his life. His firm, Capricorn Holdings, grew through its investments, buying stakes in companies engaged in oil services and crushing equipment from Combustion Engineering Inc., and a firm called Marine Drilling, which operated offshore oil rigs. Another investor in Marine Drilling was Harvard's private equity group, which oversaw the private equity investment pieces of the Harvard Endowment. Through deals in which Capricorn Holdings and Harvard were co-investors, Winokur had frequent contact with Harvard's investment managers and Harvard's endowment board. In 1995, Winokur joined the board of the Harvard Management Company, which oversees the university's endowment. In 2000, he became a member of the prestigious seven-member board of Harvard Corporation, which governs the university.

As a 2000 biography from Harvard shows, Winokur had long-standing ties with the university where he was an undergraduate, graduate, and postgraduate student. He served as a member of the Committee on University Resources, beginning in 1989, and was also a member of the advisory committee of Harvard's Mind/Brain/Behavior Initiative, as well as the Technology and Education Planning Committee of the Faculty of Arts and Sciences. Other involvement included a planning committee for Arts and Sciences faculty recruitment and development, co-chair of the reunion fundraising efforts for the Class of 1965, and a member of the New York Major Gifts Steering Committee.[2] Each of these activities showed the depth of Winokur's commitment to Harvard in terms of time, talent, and emotion. "The Harvard Management Company had four meetings a year, but you were always thinking about it. Harvard, like most institutions, is happy to have as much time as you'll give them," Winokur said with a smile.

For a while, it all went well for Winokur, with successful investments by Capricorn Holdings and time devoted to Harvard, which appreciated and benefited from his expertise as an investor. Meanwhile, Enron seemed to be growing by the proverbial leaps and bounds. Then things began to change at Enron when the company's financial façade that management presented to everyone—from shareholders to board members to Wall Street analysts—began to crumble. When things fell apart, Winokur would find himself in the crosshairs of doubt and criticism because of his service on the

Enron board. But it would be his Harvard colleagues who would deal him the cruelest blow of all.

Enron Becomes 'Unreal'

Although a complete discussion of what happened at Enron and where the company crossed the line from legitimate to illegal was beyond the scope of our interview with Winokur, he told us that, as he now sees it, Enron's undoing began when, starting in about 1999, CFO Andrew Fastow established partnerships meant to support various Enron projects. Those partnerships in hindsight proved to involve smokescreens and manipulation for certain managers' personal gain. As Bethany McLean and Peter Elkind described in their national bestseller, *The Smartest Guys in the Room: The Amazing Rise and Scandalous Fall of Enron,* "In his two years as corporate-finance czar, Fastow had employed creative forms of financial chicanery to dress up Enron's financial statements. He'd also figured out how to use his power—and his closest associates—to secretly line his own pockets. Now he established new ways to accomplish both of those ends, on a far larger scale at once."[3]

Fastow created a series of private equity funds that he named LJM (after his wife, Lea, and children, Jeffrey and Matthew), which he ran while serving as Enron's CFO. Looking back on the formation of the partnerships, Winokur recalled that they were presented to the board as legitimate, legal, and in the best interest of the company as a kind of hedge of specific investments. The board also made it clear that Fastow's compensation from the partnerships was to be modest and put controls in place as safeguards. As Winokur saw it—drawing from his own experience with Capricorn, where more than one fund sometimes invested in the same deal—there was no conflict as long as everything was disclosed properly and approved by independent third parties. Ken Lay, then CEO, and Jeffrey Skilling, who at the time was COO and eventually succeeded Lay as CEO, were required by the board to sign off on any partnership deals, and regular reports were to be made to the board's audit committee. Fastow gave assurances to the board that he was working no more than three hours a week on the funds. (Later it was disclosed that he worked almost full-time for these ventures and reaped tens of millions of dollars from them.)

Then in October 2001, Enron imploded. First, Enron announced a $544 million after-tax charge against earnings related to the company's transactions with a partnership known as LJM2, which was created and managed by Fastow. The same day, Lay announced that, because of those same transactions, shareholder equity (a key measure of a company's value) was being reduced by $1.2 billion. Those disclosures pushed Enron over the edge. Banks, investors, and traders lost confidence in the company and its reporting. Its collapse resulted in a Chapter 11 bankruptcy filing in December 2001. Enron shares that had traded at about $90 in August 2000 dropped to less than $1 when the stock was delisted in January 2002. Employees were out of their jobs and their retirement savings as portfolios dominated by the company's stock evaporated. In the wake of the Enron meltdown, Arthur Andersen, Enron's auditor, was destroyed.

As for the Enron board, some directors pointed fingers of blame at company management, especially Fastow. McLean and Elkind quoted one director who said, "The board was duped." Another noted that the board's lawyers reread every presentation made by Enron executives and concluded, "There was nothing there for the board to have reason to suspect something was wrong."[4]

As speculation swirled as to what happened and why, Winokur had his own questions that needed to be answered, which prompted him to ask to serve along with two new directors on a special investigative committee that was convened by the Enron board in October 2001. As a long-standing director and chairman of the finance committee, Winokur believed his perspective and historical knowledge would be valuable.

The special board committee's report published in February 2002 and Winokur's testimony at hearings held that same month by the House Subcommittee on Oversight and Investigation made a strong case against Enron's management for, in effect, leading the board astray. "A number of senior Enron employees, we now know, did not tell us the full truth," Winokur told Congress in his testimony.[5]

The special committee report on Enron was front-page news when it was released. The *New York Times* stated, "What emerged at Enron, as described in the report, was a culture of deception, where every effort was made to manipulate the rules and disguise the truth as part of an effort by executives to falsely pump up earnings and earn millions of dollars for themselves in the process."[6]

Although the special report clearly laid blame for the Enron debacle on the company management, the heat was still on Winokur and other board members, stoking a fire of ill-will and suspicion that had raged since the corporate meltdown had hit the headlines. As a *New York Times* writer opined, "In the clubby world of corporate boardrooms, outside directors are rarely held responsible for what befalls their companies. But as more questions emerge over the board's independence and role in the collapse of Enron, the outsiders who were Enron directors are coming under sharp criticism. And doubts are increasing over whether they will ever be named to other boards."[7]

For Winokur, the fact that he sat on the Enron board was the cause of concern for another organization, where he was also a board member: the Harvard Corporation, the governing body of Harvard University.

The Harvard Board Takes Action

By spring 2002, Enron was in the throes of bankruptcy. The report written by the special board panel had been published in early

2001, and Winokur had already gone through grilling testimony before Congress on the report's findings. In the midst of this time of relative calm, the Harvard leadership pulled the rug out from under Winokur.

Back in 2001, when Enron's troubles were splashed across the news headlines almost on a daily basis, Winokur knew his association with the company could become an embarrassment for Harvard Corporation. At the time HarvardWatch, a student-led organization, was becoming more vocal about Winokur's role on the Harvard board. As much as he loved serving on that board and was proud of his contribution, he offered to resign. His fellow board members, however, urged him to stay. It appeared at first that Harvard was sticking by him.

Then one day in April 2002, Winokur received a call from the senior fellow of the Harvard Corporation, who requested that he step down. The request seemed to come out of the blue. Winokur called Larry Summers, then president of Harvard, to work out a joint statement; Summers expressed dismay at what was happening but made no effort to reverse the decision.

What happened at Harvard was particularly hurtful for Winokur because of the way it was handled. Although no one would come out and say so, it was clear that his fellow board members wanted him off the board even though there was no evidence of wrongdoing on his part at Enron. Rather, as Enron became the poster child of corporate malfeasance, Harvard was not comfortable supporting someone associated with the Enron scandal. The only way to distance the two was for Winokur to leave the Harvard board, even though he was considered one of its most engaged members. "It felt like Murder on the Orient Express: Nobody took responsibility for it," he said.

An article in the *Harvard Crimson* in April 2002 announced Winokur's pending departure from the board, effective June 30, and noted that it "came without warning, at a moment when campus criticism of Winokur's place on the [Harvard] Corporation had subsided." The *Crimson* article included a laudatory statement from Summers about Winokur's commitment to Harvard and the time he devoted to Harvard Corporation. "Pug Winokur has been an energetic and insightful member of the Harvard Corporation, and I am saddened by the circumstances that have prompted his decision to step down. He has served Harvard with devotion and intelligence, and we owe him our gratitude for his valuable contributions to the governance of the University."

The article also quoted an unnamed university official who said Harvard Corporation members wanted to avoid the impression that they had forced Winokur to resign. "The feeling was that he should not resign in the middle of [the controversy] when charges were really flying around," the official was quoted as saying. "They didn't want it to look like Harvard was deserting Winokur."[8]

It is hard to draw any other conclusion from the board's action.

Lingering Questions

Enron's bankruptcy was long, complicated, and costly. By the end of the ordeal, Skilling was tried and convicted of fraud, and sentenced to twenty-four years and four months in prison, and Fastow, who entered a guilty plea and cooperated in the investigation, was sentenced to six years in prison. Lay was found guilty of fraud and conspiracy charges and was to be sentenced in October 2006. In July 2006, however, he died of a heart attack. A judge, following legal precedent, later revoked his conviction because Lay died before he had a chance to appeal.

As for Winokur, he was among five directors who testified before a variety of panels from Congress to creditor committees, along with John Duncan, Charles "Mickey" LeMaistre, Norman Blake, and Bob Jaedicke. Winokur spoke of his fellow directors with admiration and respect. "We were a band of brothers," he reflected.

Long after Enron faded from the news headlines, the roles and responsibilities of its board were debated by the press and other observers, particularly in context of broader discussion around corporate governance. Did the board act in good faith? Was there dereliction of duty?

Winokur's postmortem of Enron shows willful deception on the part of some top company executives. His testimony related several examples of the board being left in the dark, given false information or faulty explanations, or simply lied to. In our interview, he shook his head when relating what transpired at the company and among certain executives and those who reported to them. "Why were these people doing this?" he said. "So many people were in on the game internally." He described one risk management executive at Enron who testified publicly after Enron's bankruptcy that he didn't like some of the hedges that the company was using. "I met with him several times in private," Winokur said. "He had plenty of time to say something to me, but never did."

In his testimony, Winokur also acknowledged widespread criticism leveled at the board, in particular for approving Fastow's partnerships. "Those criticisms have hit us hard, because I firmly believed at the time—and believe today—that the board made the business judgment to permit Mr. Fastow to serve in these partnerships for one reason and one reason only. Based upon the information presented to us, and upon the advice of our outside auditors and lawyers, we believed these transactions would be in the best interests of Enron and its shareholders. That this turned out to be untrue has been devastating to all of us."

Winokur conceded in his testimony that the other two members of the special committee, without his participation and with the benefit of hindsight, disagreed with some of the decisions made by the board. However, he told Congress, "They offer no suggestion that the board did not act honestly and in good faith in approving these structures." Winokur also voiced support for his colleagues on the board, calling them "highly accomplished in their fields . . . highly intelligent, and, I believe, highly ethical as well."

"As a board, we worked well as a unit to help move Enron forward into a new business environment characterized by increased globalization of investment, rapid regulatory and technological change, and increased sophistication in the capital markets," Winokur told Congress. He added that although Enron took business and financial risks, these risks were disclosed in financial information that it filed with the SEC, and also were known to analysts and rating agencies following the company.[9]

It was not the board's responsibility to look over every facet of the company's business, Winokur maintained; that job is management's. As he told the Congressional subcommittee, "The reality in the modern corporation is that directors cannot, and are not expected to, manage a company on a day-to-day basis. Rather, to be a director is to direct. As directors our role was to inform general corporate policy and to approve Enron management's strategic goals. We were required to do so on an informed basis, in good faith, and in the honest belief that the actions we took were in the best interest of Enron."[10]

Bethany McLean, co-author of the bestselling book on Enron's rise and fall, called the issue of board responsibility "a difficult question." McLean, who covered Enron for *Fortune* magazine, admitted that she had changed her mind over the years, particularly as she's gotten to know Winokur since Enron. "At one point I would have been far more critical of the board," she said. "Now I have an appreciation of how difficult it is to be a board member. You have to believe in management and you have to trust management to a certain extent. You can't do everything yourself. If you don't admire and have faith in management then you better get off the board. And yet, you also have to have a degree of skepticism. How do you find the right balance between admiration and skepticism?"

What complicated matters for Enron's board was the complexity of the company—with its international assets, diverse ventures such as broadband, volatile trading operations, and intricate partnerships—which was made even more complicated by efforts of management to cloak what was really happening inside the firm. "You can look back with the benefit of hindsight and say, 'Why didn't the board ask more questions?' but at the time it was much more difficult," McLean added.

McLean said Winokur strikes her as "someone who would not be derelict in his duties or ever willingly compromise himself." What's interesting to see, she added, "is how someone whose character is so good can end up in a situation that, with the benefit of hindsight, isn't so good."

Winokur has taken his first-hand experience of just how difficult it can be to serve as an outside director and offered it as advice to first-time board members. As he wrote in an August 2009 article for *Directorship*, "You now must consider reputational risk, substantially expanded (and often last minute) time commitments—perhaps at little per diem pay—and much increased formalism (which can impinge on candid strategic focus). Make sure you understand the pros and cons and do your due diligence on both the company and its industry, as you will be judged in the court of public opinion—and perhaps even in the courthouse. You will need courage, good business instincts, and the rare ability to judge others accurately."[11]

After the Storm

In perfect hindsight, Winokur acknowledged, he might have resigned from Enron when he was chosen for the Harvard Corporation board in 2000. That would have avoided the mess he faced a year later. However, if he had left the Enron board, he most likely would have sold his stock, since he would no longer have been a current director. "And if I had done that," Winokur explained, "people would have said to me, 'you knew.'" Not selling his stock, he said, "proved to be a great thing"—providing further evidence that he did not know what was happening with the company.

Throughout the ordeal what was most upsetting to Winokur were the media reports that he viewed as inaccurate. "They kept writing stuff that was factually wrong," he said. For example, some reports intimated that Winokur had made millions by selling Enron stock, but his public filings showed that he never sold a share prior to Enron's bankruptcy. Winokur believes directors should hold their company shares throughout their time on the board and not sell them until some time has passed after their board terms are over.

The harsh glare of negative media attention was particularly hard on Winokur's wife, Dee, and his two adult daughters, Annick and Andra. "Before Enron I was never in the press—ever. Then all of a sudden there was this starburst of bad stuff, and they didn't like it," Winokur said of his family. Their support of him, however, was unshakeable.

Winokur has peace of mind knowing that he never engaged in any wrongdoing and was never accused of any illegality. "I feel like I've been to the world's most thorough proctologist, who found nothing wrong with me regarding Enron," Winokur quipped.

Moreover, the fact remains that no matter how much one might wish to be able to erase a traumatic episode, it is impossible to alter the past. Rather, the choice is to learn from it and to move on to the best of one's ability. For Winokur, top of the list of the things he learned was who his friends are—a wider circle of connections that now includes lawyers he met during the Enron ordeal who have become personal friends.

Other lessons learned encompass testing his own character and affirming his principles, including his sense of right and wrong, which he attributed to his family and upbringing. He recalled a lesson in ethics from his boyhood when he and a friend found a wallet full of money in a field. The boys decided to split the money and tossed the wallet aside. When his friend's mother found a stash of money, the story came out. At the parents' insistence, the boys combed the field to look for the wallet, which they found. When an ad placed in the newspaper caught the eye of the owner—a sailor on leave who had saved up his "getting married money"—young Winokur and his friend learned a valuable lesson about right and wrong. "If you are raised to do the right thing, business ethics are not that complicated," Winokur observed.

From the Enron turmoil, Winokur walked away with valuable lessons that could only be learned in the midst of catastrophe, which he readily shares with others who might be facing similar trauma through no fault of their own. "You learn it's not about you at all. If you are in the middle of it, you're in a storm. There's nothing you can do. You have to accept that it's not about you at all," Winokur said, quoting a friend's advice given to him in 2001. "When you are there, though, it's hard to accept that. It does feel like it's about you. There is that period of time when people are wondering about you a little bit. The people who know you, though, don't wonder. The people who don't know you, they're the ones who wonder."

New Ventures and Unfinished Business

Enron sidetracked Winokur, but did not derail him. With more time available to him after leaving the Enron and Harvard boards, Winokur decided to devote his energy and resources to promote the public good and to undertake one pet project in particular that was the direct result of his frustration from the Enron experience. Upset with the way the press reported the Enron story, which often repeated and perpetuated errors, Winokur founded The Audit (http://www.cjr.org/the_audit/), a venture overseen by Columbia University's Journalism School. Through The Audit, Winokur has brought together other backers and members of the business press to encourage discussion of how business issues are reported by journalists. "I did that as a way to deal constructively with my anger toward the business press," he added.

McLean, who is among the journalists involved in The Audit, agreed that the media did come down very hard on the Enron board, and included herself in those ranks. The problem is that when a far-reaching and complex news story is unfolding, journalists can only rely on the facts and information they have, which may be incomplete or even one-sided. When journalists reach out to corporate officials who will not talk to the press regarding issues involving their companies, news stories will reflect only the facts at hand. "In the media when you have a fact pattern and an investigative report from the government that appears to corroborate that fact pattern—and you call board members and they are not talking—you only know those facts," McLean added.

Winokur also became a director of Ithaka (www.ithaka.org), a not-for-profit organization that has established a digital archive to advance research and support the scholarly community, originally organized by the Andrew W. Mellon Foundation. With his older daughter, Annick, who was a graduate student in Yale's pediatric nurse practitioner program, Winokur started Squash Haven (www.squashhaven.org), which promotes academic, athletic, and personal growth for young people in New Haven, Connecticut, modeled after similar programs in Boston and New York.

The project closest to his heart is one that Winokur and his wife, Dee, established in the Mississippi Delta, called Delta Directions (www.deltadirections.org). This project had its beginnings from a golfing trip for Winokur and his then eighty-five-year-old mother, Marjorie "Marge" Winokur, and a chance meeting with actor Morgan Freeman at the restaurant he owns in Clarksdale, Mississippi, with business partner Bill Luckett. After Marge told Freeman that her mother was a friend of the real "Miss Daisy" (the subject of the movie, *Driving Miss Daisy*, co-starring Freeman), the actor extended an invitation to his local blues club for drinks and a game of pool. A conversation ensued around their interests in the South.

On the way back home, Winokur and his mother discussed the needs of the region, which led to his commitment to spark renewal in the area. Winokur reached out to a college friend, Dr. Barry Smith, who runs the Dreyfus Health Foundation, telling him that if the foundation began a program in the Delta, Winokur and his wife would help provide funding. Since then, Delta Directions has grown to include many strategic partners, thanks in large part to Winokur's many connections. For example, with partial funding from Winokur, Harvard and Mississippi State University joined forces to establish a two-year fellowship that staffs a Harvard Law School graduate as a full-time "Delta Fellow" in the region. Students from Harvard Law and that university's School of Public Health get hands-on experience in public service and economic development projects and course credit through the Winokur family's Delta activities.

The list of academic partners has also grown to include about five or six universities interested in undertaking academic research in the Delta and applying for federal grants to underwrite research programs. Initiatives undertaken have included nursing leadership and programs created toward improving maternal and infant health, training of newly elected African American officials, establishing community farmers' markets, and providing microfinancing and technical assistance to newly formed businesses. "The needs and opportunities in the Mississippi Delta are so overwhelming," added Winokur, who is personally involved with his university partners in setting priorities for many of the projects. "We're trying to get more people engaged in what we do."

The philanthropic and social service projects are a positive postscript on an exceedingly difficult period for Winokur. They are also reflective of his younger, idealistic days in Washington when the agenda was that of the Great Society. What's made it possible now is his success in business and his many connections to people and resources.

At times, however, a storm leaves unfinished business. It seems clear from the conversation with Winokur that his feelings about how his colleagues on the Harvard Corporation treated him are not fully resolved. Although he is on good terms with current Harvard leadership and parts of Harvard have been enthusiastic participants in the Delta projects, Winokur admitted, in response to a question about leaving the Harvard Corporation, "I have to decide how to put it behind me." In time, Winokur's breach from Harvard may be resolved, or it may remain unaddressed. His story is a reminder that as wounds heal scars will remain, but new growth is possible.

Yet as Winokur demonstrates, even when things turn ugly there can be benefits, from self-knowledge to discovering one's priorities. "My view is the storm will enable you to find your roots, to find your base, to find out how centered you are," he reflected. "People will do it their own way. I will do that through my friends and family. Anything that shakes your life makes you look deeply, to figure out why you are here. It makes you come back from it and find out what's important."

I'm on this earth for a short period of time
and I want to make a difference.

—HARRY KRAEMER,
FORMER CHAIRMAN AND CEO,
BAXTER INTERNATIONAL

Chapter Six

HARRY M. JANSEN KRAEMER, JR.
VALUES-BASED LEADERSHIP

For twenty-two years, Harry M. Jansen Kraemer, Jr. made Baxter International Inc. his corporate home, from his first position as a director of corporate development in 1982 to becoming CEO in 1999—a position he held for nearly six years. Although he identified strongly with the company and felt a personal connection with employees, Kraemer took pains not to become wrapped up in the trappings of being a CEO. A philosophy of life and leadership that puts greater emphasis on family and values such as spirituality, humility, and making a difference helped Kraemer keep his job from consuming him.

"I never allowed myself to get caught up in it," he reflected. "There are so many things you don't control. When I was appointed CEO, I knew the average CEO is in the job three or four years. I said, 'I'm going to enjoy this. I'm always going to do the right thing and do the best I can. And what happens, happens.'"

Establishing a healthy separation between his title and his sense of self enabled Kraemer, fifty-four, to clearly see his way about who he was and what his priorities were—especially where his family was concerned. He continually engaged in self-reflection, a practice he established in high school and one of the four main principles of his philosophy of values-based leadership. This philosophy has guided Kraemer's career since the beginning and continues to influence his personal and professional choices today.

Self-reflection is so important to Kraemer that he considers it to be the foundation of his leadership. As he wrote in a first-person discussion on leadership: "In my opinion, 99 percent of us are just racing around and in constant motion, and not really taking the time to think. Until you actually take the time to slow down and ask yourself what you think are the real key questions, it's very difficult to wrap your arms around anything."[1]

Kraemer's second leadership principle is balance, which to him means more than the phrase "work/life balance." Rather, he sees it more broadly as the ability to integrate family, career, spirituality, health, fun, and being socially responsible—that is, being what Kraemer calls "a best citizen." As a CEO and father of five children, Kraemer exhibited the ability to balance it all—from soccer games to Sunday school—and still run the company.

Kraemer described his third principle as "true self-confidence," a key component of leadership, which is more than acting a certain way or playing a role. Rather, it stems from self-reflection and self-assessment and leads to more authentic leadership. "It means knowing I'm far from perfect, but I know I am okay and I am comfortable in my own skin. I know what I know, and I know what I don't know. I'm a learning person and I know I will improve with each and every day I am given."

Lastly, the principle of genuine humility. Kraemer summed it up as "never forgetting where you came from." Genuine humility not only keeps the ego in check, which Kraemer sees as essential the higher one advances, but it also helps leaders identify with those who report to him or her. Team members (Kraemer does not like the term "employees"), in turn, will know that the leader really does appreciate and remember what it's like to work on a lower rung of the proverbial corporate ladder. As Kramer explained, people will more willingly follow leaders they can relate to. Employees constantly look to the leader to see if he or she is approachable and truly cares about them.

Kraemer used this leadership philosophy to guide his career over the years at Baxter, from his first job in 1982 as director of corporate development, through the ranks of the corporation, to the CEO office in 1999. His four leadership principles also became essential when he faced a sudden upset in his professional life and then needed to chart a new course for himself.

The Balanced Life

Talking about his career, Kraemer segued easily into a discussion about his leadership principles, which he writes and speaks about frequently. The principles are second nature to him, whether he is chronicling how he transitioned from one job to the next over the years or discussing advice he provides to graduate students who are contemplating their careers. Throughout the discussion, he demonstrated his belief that people should be grounded in whatever they determine to be most important in life; in his case his faith and family. As Kraemer summed it up, echoing his self-talk, "Yes, you've done well, Harry, but you must never forget where you came from. You have some skills and you've worked hard. But you need to take the time to realize that there is also a lot of luck involved and an unbelievable amount of timing. And I know there is somebody 'upstairs' who is directing all this."

Kraemer's career path was smooth. After receiving his MBA from Kellogg in 1979, Kraemer worked for Northwest Industries before joining Baxter in 1982. Over the next two decades, he held positions of increasing responsibility at Baxter in domestic and international operations, including senior vice president and chief financial officer in 1993, president of Baxter in 1997, and then CEO in 1999, with the additional title of chairman in January 2000 as he took over from retiring top executive Vernon Loucks, Jr.

During Kraemer's tenure as CFO and later as CEO, Baxter experienced strong growth, both internally and through acquisitions. Realizing its strategic vision, Baxter expanded as a global player in the pharmaceutical and health care industry. A 2002 *BusinessWeek* profile highlighted Baxter's 1997 purchase of Immuno AG, as well as several other deals. Through these actions, Baxter expanded its line of plasma-derived and recombinant therapeutic proteins; added new wound-management and vaccine products, as well as technologies to carry oxygen to vital organs and to develop technologies to inactivate viral pathogens in collected blood; and strengthened its market presence and research and development capabilities, especially in Europe. While impressive, these feats were not the focus of the *BusinessWeek* profile. Instead, the article described how Kraemer, despite his CEO position, made his family his priority. "He has just settled his infant son, Daniel, in a portable crib in the kitchen and is now hopping into his car to pick up daughter Shannon, 8, from First Communion practice. At the church, he bumps into another dad, who is organizing a weekend camping trip that Kraemer has been planning to take with Shannon. Back home, he checks in with his oldest, 14-year-old Suzie, and then takes over from wife Julie in supervising the other two kids—Andrew, 11, and Diane, 4—who are bouncing on a backyard trampoline he bought at Sam's Club. In a moment, Kraemer, 47, is springing into the air, too."[2]

Kraemer won accolades for his advocacy of a balanced life, which he encouraged in employees and modeled himself: leaving his office by 6:00 P.M. when he was not traveling so he could head home for dinner with his wife and five children. From 6:00 to 9:00 P.M. was family time, and then he would jog for an hour. From 10:00 P.M. to 1 A.M. he did his reading, e-mail, and voicemail. As he saw it, many things could be accomplished as long as he kept his life in equilibrium with discipline, focus, consistency, and credibility.

His campaign for better life balance, the *BusinessWeek* article noted, was also good for business. Since 1993, when Kraemer became CFO, Baxter hit its earnings growth target each quarter—even as it nearly doubled its profit goal, to a growth rate of 15 percent. Its gross margin hit a record 44.8 percent and market capitalization increased more than tenfold to $35.7 billion over eight and a half years. Although a family-first policy did not directly produce Baxter's strong performance, the *BusinessWeek* article did see a link: By encouraging employees to adopt a schedule that best fit their needs, Baxter was able to attract and recruit top people. And the time spent at work was higher quality because people weren't as distracted by what was happening at home. In the article, Kraemer attributed his convictions and leadership lessons to his father, who was a businessman: "His whole focus was the family. I don't think he ever went out without taking at least one or two of us along."[3]

William J. White, retired chairman and CEO of Bell & Howell Company and a professor in the Department of Industrial Engineering and Management Sciences at Northwestern University, praised Kraemer for having the discipline to maintain a balanced life. One way to achieve that, he counseled, is to rely on a trusted adviser such as a spouse, friend, sibling, or close associate—particularly someone who can be counted on to provide honest feedback. "The trusted adviser will help you keep your balance among different aspects of your life such as career, family, faith, and so forth," White added. "When you have that balance, then if you suffer a setback in one area of your life such as your career, you have two or three others to fall back on."

For Kraemer, his wife, Julie, has been his trusted adviser throughout his career. With her support, he put values-based leadership first, especially the principle of "genuine humility" and not forgetting where he came from. "I was always surprised when I was told I was going to be promoted. In almost every instance, Julie would say, 'I'm very proud of you being promoted, but I love you regardless of your title. Can we still be normal people and not get caught up in the position or title?' I would respond to

Julie, 'We haven't changed our life view since we were 21 years old so I don't think I will change now. However, if I do start to forget, I am sure that you will encourage me to walk away from it,'" he recalled.

Leadership in Action

As a top executive, Kraemer was not only well regarded for leading the company through periods of high performance while championing balanced lifestyles for employees, but he also received high marks from some of his would-be critics. In 1998, a group of activist investors—the advocacy group Healthcare Without Harm—filed a shareholder resolution demanding that Baxter phase out production of polyvinyl chloride (PVC) plastic, which was used in IVs, blood bags, and dialysis tubing. Kraemer, who was then president and would become CEO in two months, invited the group to the company's headquarters in Deerfield, Illinois, to meet with top executives. "They allowed an open, heated dialogue that made all of us smarter," Charlotte Brody, head of Healthcare Without Harm," told *Chief Executive* magazine. "They had the people who could make the decisions at the table . . . It wasn't just public relations and investor relations [people] to politely disregard everything we had to say." Baxter agreed to set a phase-out schedule for its PVC products and refrain from letting PVC trade groups include Baxter in advertising. In return, the activists withdrew their resolution.[4]

Perhaps the biggest test of Kraemer's leadership came in 2001, after fifty-three people died following kidney dialysis using a Baxter blood filter. For Kraemer, it was a "moment of truth," wrote *Fast Company* magazine in October 2002. "How Baxter responded would leave a lasting imprint on the company's relationships with patients and doctors, with employees, and, of course, with investors. The episode would, for better or worse, open a window onto Baxter's corporate soul."[5] That soul was very much under the influence of Kraemer, who took responsibility for the incident, as well as an after-tax charge of $156 million. Although the company met its 2001 financial targets—which would have entitled Kraemer and other top executives to annual bonuses of up to 150 percent of their base pay—Kraemer urged the board to cut their payouts. Kraemer slashed his own compensation more severely than anyone else's. "The buck stops somewhere, and in this case, it stops here," he told *BusinessWeek*.[6]

Through such actions, Kraemer solidified his reputation as an ethical CEO with a strong moral compass. As *Fast Company* noted, "What separates Kraemer from most CEOs you've read about is this: He is relentlessly authentic. He tells the truth, and he acts on his beliefs." The article also quoted Donald P. Jacobs, dean emeritus at Northwestern University's Kellogg School of Management, who said: "There are relatively few people in the world like Harry. Harry lives his life the way most of us would like to live our lives. What Harry says he believes in, you can put it in the bank. The way he treats his coworkers is the way he'd like people to treat him."[7]

Speaking with high energy and passion, Kraemer described numerous examples of values-based leadership in action, which also helped him keep a healthy separation from his personal identity and his job title, particularly when he became CEO. After taking Baxter's twelve-seater Falcon 900 jet on a business excursion to Europe, Asia, or Latin America, to keep things in balance he would take a commercial flight for the next trip—typically flying in coach class. "Everybody would tease me: I was the CEO at Baxter, but I lived in the same house as when I was a senior analyst and I drove a six-year-old Toyota."

When visiting with employees in the United States and internationally, Kraemer never differentiated among people by title or responsibility. "I didn't treat you as an executive vice president any differently than if you were a summer intern," he said. "I would sit and have lunch with the assistants and clerical teams. I would go into a plant, walk in the front door, and visit all 600 people—shake hands and have lunch in the cafeteria. And then I'd tell the plant manager, 'Let's go buy seventy or eighty gallons of ice cream, buy some funny hats, and you and I can scoop ice cream in the afternoon for all of our team members.'"

Such actions were not gimmicks but expressions of his leadership. In turn, others perceived Kraemer as genuine because his behavior was consistent over more than two decades of working in the same environment. Harry Kraemer CEO was no different in their eyes than Harry Kraemer corporate employee—a lesson he summed up as "remember the cube!" referring to the cubicle (or laboratory bench or field sales rep's car) where most people start their careers. As he saw it, not forgetting any of those early experiences was the key to living a balanced life and tangible proof of his leadership in action.

When Results Disappoint

Given the amount of praise Kraemer received as CFO, president, and then CEO of Baxter, one might have expected him to enjoy a long tenure as the top executive. But things began to change in 2002, which Baxter called a very challenging year. As Kraemer wrote in the annual report for that year, while the compounded annual rate of return to shareholders increased 25 percent from 1993 to 2001, Baxter's stock price dropped by 47 percent in 2002, compared with declines of 23 percent in the S&P 500 and 20 percent in the S&P 500 Health Care Index. Many companies were experiencing volatility in the stock market at the time, but Baxter was also under pressure from increased competition in the United States, particularly for its plasma-derived therapeutic products and slower growth in its renal business. As a result Baxter had to lower its sales growth expectations.[8] In 2003, Baxter saw a decline in income from continuing operations, although net income was higher. Moreover, as Kraemer told shareholders in the 2003 annual report, results fell short of the earnings target it set for itself at the beginning of the year.[9]

These disappointments followed a long run of strong earnings at Baxter, which had been called "one of the industry's best and most consistent growth machines" by *BusinessWeek*.[10] This is not uncommon among companies that post strong growth over an extended period. Still, instead of praise, Kraemer now faced questions, including from his own board. Kraemer recalled that when Baxter had to reduce its earnings forecasts more than once in 2003, it prompted an inquiry from the Securities and Exchange Commission (SEC). But he wasn't worried about the SEC. "The CFO in me said, 'The SEC is simply doing their job by asking questions,'" Kraemer remembered. Looking back, however, he acknowledged that he may not have fully appreciated directors' nervousness in what was then the new era of Sarbanes-Oxley regulations regarding financial reporting. Kraemer also expressed self-criticism over the way he handled concerns from board members because he believed there was nothing fundamentally wrong with the company or its operations. In hindsight, he believes he should have been more sensitive to the board's concerns.

An issue with the SEC never materialized. Nonetheless, discussions with the board escalated to the point that it was suggested Kraemer should consider resigning. "I don't think I really absorbed that comment—the fact that they would ask me to leave since the company had done so well for so many years," he recalled. "But the bottom line was I was leaving Baxter."

For the man who lived and breathed Baxter, it was an unexpected and emotional ending. Very little of it played out in the press. In fact, news of Kraemer's resignation as chairman and CEO in late January 2004 earned just a few paragraphs, compared to lengthy articles that had lauded his leadership. The *New York Times* published a brief write-up announcing that Kraemer was resigning as chairman and CEO: "Mr. Kraemer, 49, cited the challenges Baxter had faced during the last year as the reason for his departure."[11]

Kraemer's career at Baxter—spanning nearly half his lifetime—had come to an end. Looking back, the most emotional issue for Kraemer was leaving a company that he loved after twenty-two years and employees who felt like family. "I remember thinking to myself, 'Hey, I'm fine. I am a very fortunate and blessed fellow.' . . . But I really worried about these 50,000 team members. I remember telling two board members, 'Since you don't have someone who is immediately prepared to succeed me, I am willing to continue in the CEO position until you have the right person in place.' That's exactly what I did."

Such commitment—offering to remain highly involved in day-to-day activities for months after being asked to resign in order to ensure a smooth transition—is rare for any executive. "This was not one of those, 'He's going to stay for a couple of months—wink, wink.' I conducted all of the key meetings and plan reviews," Kraemer said. "I was there for everything. I wanted to stay true to my mantra: I will do the right thing and do the best I can."

What was most painful for Kraemer, perhaps, was the responsibility he felt to those who had joined the company because of him and who stayed because they enjoyed working with him. "Many of these people were at Baxter because of me and I was leaving them—and I wasn't leaving on my own choice," Kraemer explained. "That became tougher when many of them said, 'If you're leaving, we're leaving.' I encouraged them to do what was best for them, and many of them decided to stay."

After the new CEO took over, however, a new team was recruited, which is typical in a management change. Soon many of those whom Kraemer had urged to stay with Baxter were being asked to depart. Nearly five years later, the only regret Kraemer voiced was for these colleagues—never for himself. His overall attitude was one of gratitude for the opportunities he had been given. "When I heard a board member say, 'Maybe you should leave,' I was shocked, but I didn't get into whether it was fair. I had been fortunate to become the CEO of a major global company, a position that 99.9 percent of people never have the opportunity to experience," he noted.

Given his longstanding practice of self-reflection, it was no surprise that Kraemer quickly reached for the positive. Even in the company's announcement that he was resigning as CEO Kraemer said he "felt blessed to have been part of the Baxter team . . . "[12] Today Kraemer still expresses those sentiments. "I truly loved my twenty-two years at Baxter. If I hadn't left the company at that point, I might still be there. Now, in hindsight, I realize that if I had stayed I never would have experienced all of the remarkable things I now have the opportunity to do."

Departures and Life Lessons

After his resignation from Baxter, Kraemer's transition was not automatic, nor was it without emotional upset. However, as he processed the events and asked himself what he could have done differently, Kraemer said he learned to avoid the "shoulda, coulda, woulda" thinking that can keep a person locked in the past—a lesson he underscores for anyone who is undergoing the postmortem of a previous job. "Now you're in the present and going into the future," he added. "Learn from the past, but don't dwell on it."

He summarized another lesson learned from undergoing a career upheaval by quoting M. Scott Peck's *The Road Less Traveled*: "Life is difficult." Understanding that fact helps to avoid victimhood and blame when things suddenly turn for the worse. For Kraemer, such insight reinforces the need for continual self-reflection, without which he believes it's nearly impossible to stay grounded, weather the difficulties, and make the best choices for the future.

Today, Kraemer's professional and avocational life is divided into three parts: as a clinical professor of management and strategy at Northwestern University's Kellogg School of Management; as an executive partner at private equity firm Madison Dearborn Partners based in Chicago; and as a member of some thirteen boards, including as chairman of the board at his undergraduate alma mater, Lawrence University in Appleton, Wisconsin. As he discovered, "If your goal is to be an example and have influence on as many people as you possibly can, and if you have a fairly curious mindset and a low threshold for boredom, you can collect activities that will engage you as much as or more than when you were CEO."

New Beginnings

Admittedly, after leaving Baxter, Kraemer's first assumption was that he would find another company to run. "The initial thought was I have to jump into something quick because I'm going to be bored quickly." Plus, Kraemer had seen a CEO role as the best way to put his values-based leadership into practice and set a positive example for a team. However, he realized that going into the top job of a new organization would be far different from his experience at Baxter of rising through the ranks to become CEO. "I thought, well, maybe I could do the CEO-thing again. However, Julie and I decided we would go through a complete life plan exercise and consider what all the alternatives were," he said.

As Kraemer contemplated his options, he avoided jumping at the first opportunity to come along. Instead, he engaged in a purposeful, soul-searching transition with the support of his wife. What came next was not another CEO post. His decision was to pursue a "potpourri of activities," as he described it; diverse interests and activities that allow him to make a difference. "I was very fortunate in leaving Baxter. Rather than going 180 miles per hour, Julie and I said, 'Let's take the time to think this through.'"

Among the first opportunities to arise for Kraemer was teaching at Northwestern University's Kellogg School of Management. When he was approached about teaching, Kraemer had little interest in instructing students in areas of his technical expertise such as finance. Instead, he proposed teaching values-based leadership, along with curricula that address mergers and acquisitions and leading a global company. Today, his students include those in the full-time and part-time programs; those in the two-year executive MBA program that is taught on weekends, and also the Kellogg Miami Executive MBA Program, which caters to students from South and Central America who fly to Florida once a month for intensive instruction.

What was most appealing about teaching was the ability to pass on his experience and philosophy to "the next generation of people who are going to lead organizations around the world," Kraemer said. "To help them learn what values-based leadership is really all about—self-reflection and balance—I thought this could be great."

Teaching also put Kraemer back in the leadership spotlight. In 2007, the *Chicago Tribune* featured the former CEO in the classroom full of MBA students at Kellogg "hanging on his every word." As the article stated, "Nearly three years after he lost the top job at health-care giant Baxter International Inc., Kraemer is trying to convert the next generation of corporate leaders to his do-the-right-thing management style. His evangelism comes at a time when hundreds of major companies are mired in stock option scandals and shareholder outrage over CEO compensation—and enormous golden parachutes—continues to grow."[13]

As part of his varied activities, Kraemer also found another audience for his message: the executives he counsels through the private equity firm where he is an executive partner. Before he agreed to join any organization, however, he wanted to assess the fit according to his values-based philosophy, which must have come as a surprise in some corners of the business world. While still in the "exploratory, life-planning phase," Kraemer met with many private equity firms in New York about the possibility of joining them, but the value alignment was not there. For example, when Kraemer explained that he was teaching leadership classes at Kellogg two days a week, the response was, "You can get out of that, right?" His reply: "No, in fact, that's what I got into. I love teaching!"

Shortly thereafter, Kraemer was approached by Tim Sullivan, one of the founding partners of Madison Dearborn, whom Kraemer had met when they taught Sunday school together at their local church. After initial discussions, he realized that this opportunity to join Madison Dearborn could work because of the firm's strong alignment with his values and life balance. "When I said to them, 'I only want to do this two days a week,' I did not get that MEGO— My-Eyes-Glaze-Over look . . . They were telling me, try it for three months and you tell us." Kraemer joined Madison Dearborn as an executive partner in 2005 and has been with the firm ever since.

Kraemer draws upon his own experiences as a former CFO and a CEO as he works with the top executives running the companies in which Madison Dearborn is a private-equity investor. For example, remembering his days of visiting the field when he was the head of Baxter, Kraemer advised one executive during a plant visit to spend as much time as possible with all employees. He told him, "We don't need to sit in a conference room and watch a PowerPoint presentation that we can read back at the office. We only visit this plant in this town once a year. You have 700 team members here. Don't you think they would want to see you? Let's go around and shake hands with all 700 people." Following Kraemer's example, that's exactly what the executive did.

Kraemer has also become actively involved on the boards of public companies, private companies, and not-for-profit organizations. During his time at Baxter, he admitted, "I was somewhat involved in outside boards, but not as much as I wanted to. I focused on Baxter, my family, and my faith. That really meant that anything outside of those three areas couldn't happen to any significant degree."

Previously, serving on the board at Lawrence University meant attending meetings, but rarely signing up for committees or other projects—and often standing in the hallway texting and retrieving messages on his Blackberry or taking cell phone calls. Today he is more actively involved and serves as chairman of Lawrence

University and of NorthShore University HealthSystem in the northern Chicago suburbs, where all five of his children were born.

Kraemer admitted that the life he has now is not what he intended ten years earlier when he ascended to the top position at Baxter. "I must admit I would not have predicted this. In fact, it's unbelievable to me now. When I get calls from recruiters who ask, 'Would you consider becoming a CEO again?' my reaction is, 'Boy, that would be so limiting. It would just be one company, in one industry, compared to the much more global perspective I have today.' I wouldn't have thought that would be the case five years ago."

Sharing Life Lessons

As Kraemer described the activities that engage him today, he exhibited particular passion for sharing his experiences and views with students, helping them discern for themselves what the best career move might be. "We can have a discussion of what's important to them and what are their values," Kraemer said, segueing into a scenario. "You just got married and you and your spouse want to have a baby, but you're talking about this job in New York and traveling 90 percent of the time. You may decide to do it, but have you thought through all the life experiences? . . . I've got to tell you, we have many amazing discussions that make a difference in people's lives."

When students sometimes state that they need to devote themselves 100 percent to their job for the first five or six years before they can start thinking about life balance, Kraemer poses probing questions, but leaves it to students to make their own decisions. His habit is not to engage in question-and-answer sessions with them; rather, as he describes it, in "questions and opinions" sessions.

"I'll say, I have a few questions for you to think about. First, how can you focus 100 percent on your job and forget everything else? How do you forget your spouse's birthday or decide to celebrate it next month? Or you miss Joey learning to crawl, but your spouse can make a video. And how do you decide when it's time to start focusing on these things? How do you turn that knob off? Do you try to be more balanced when you become a director or a vice president? You don't know the end point," Kraemer reflected. "How do you deal with all the things you trivialized? How do you get excited about the fourth grade soccer game when you've missed the first, second, and third grade games?"

Kraemer drew upon the experiences of former classmates at Kellogg, about half of whom ended up getting divorced, including many who "don't even know what happened." He described having his students imagine what it would be like to have their spouse inform them that they were not waiting around for them anymore, or having a son or daughter say, "You were never around for the last seven or eight years, so I prefer you not to start coming to my games now that it is suddenly convenient for you. I don't even know who you are." He added: "When I say these things in a class of 30-year-olds, you can hear a pin drop."

As he also teaches his students, Kraemer believes that life balance plays a role in good corporate governance, helping to ensure that people's attachment to their jobs titles, salaries, and perquisites will not cloud their judgment. Drawing a line on a piece of paper, he repeated an example given to his class at Kellogg. The line represented the demarcation between what is legal and what is not. "What about when it's close to the line? It's legal, but is it the right thing?" Kraemer asked. "The way I describe it is you never want to get even close to the line. First, the line is not well marked and, second, the line often moves. Before you know it, you are on the other side of the line. And then what do you do?"

Beware the Speeding Porsche

Kraemer's lessons are not exclusively for his students. He has readily shared his experiences and opinions with former CEOs, including those who were asked to resign. Often they contact him to gather information about how he made the transition to teaching, private equity, and boards. Kraemer's first message to them, however, is not to make a move too quickly, but rather to spend time to process the transition and discern what comes next.

"You have to take some time to really stop and think through what you are all about. Where do you want to go? I call it self-reflection. What are your goals and what are your values? Maybe you are 55 and in good health. God willing, you may live to 80. What is important to you, your spouse, and your family? I am not one of those guys who at 60 years old is going to play golf. I want to find a portfolio of activities in which I can set an example and make a difference and do it for 25 or 30 years," Kraemer reflected.

He compared the life of many CEOs to the analogy of racing along at 200 miles per hour in a Porsche—going virtually nonstop 24/7—and then suddenly coming to a halt. A moment later, the car is gone. "Your first thought is, 'I've got to get another car, another Porsche, to start moving really fast again.' But maybe it's time for a different car or to get on the bus. What are all the other things you could do?"

The people who "get it," Kraemer said, are typically those who tend to be self-reflective, self-aware, and spiritual. "With certain people you will engage in some fairly philosophical discussions." For others, Kraemer's opinions have little or no impact because the focus is all about being behind the wheel of the proverbial Porsche again. "If you just get into another Porsche and you don't take time to reflect, you're just spinning," he remarked. "I'm talking about something very different—constantly thinking, 'How will this impact what I do tomorrow? How will I become a better person, a better leader, and interact differently with others?'"

Admittedly, when he discusses the concept of life balance with other former CEOs, not everyone accepts the message. "I'll divide the world into two groups: those who say, 'I don't know what you're talking about. I've got to find another job quickly,' and others who say, 'You're saying some things that sound very important to me. I can relate to what you are saying,'" Kraemer explained.

Using the principles of values-based leadership, Kraemer has embraced the next phase of his life with enthusiasm, even to the point of seeing the Baxter board's request for his resignation as a gift that has enabled him to broaden his sphere of influence. Furthermore, the principles have become a foundation as he strives to be a positive influence on others: from his Kellogg students who will be the future global leaders, the executives of Madison Dearborn portfolio companies, and the various organizations on which he serves as a board member.

Since undergoing his own transition, Kraemer has become an example for others. His message is also a caution to those who, in the midst of change or upset, may be tempted to jump to a new opportunity too soon before taking the time to reflect on what they've learned, what their values are, what is important to them, and how they want to spend the next phase of their lives.

Achieving the lofty rank of CEO, Kraemer moved in elite circles from the Conference Board, where he sat down regularly with former Federal Reserve Chairman Paul Volcker, to the World Economic Forum held annually in Davos, Switzerland. And yet his proudest accomplishment had nothing to do with his corporate life. Rather, it came quite by surprise.

It was June 2008, and the faculty and students at Kellogg were gathered to celebrate the end of the school year. Kraemer, who had been unable to attend the previous year's event, was pleased to join the festivities, talk with students and colleagues, and enjoy a glass of wine. Then it was time for the announcement of the recipient of the L.G. Lavengood Outstanding Professor of the Year Award, honoring a professor chosen by graduating members of the full-time and part-time Kellogg MBA programs.

When Kraemer heard his name, he was overwhelmed. "It was the proudest moment of my life," he said—even more than being named CEO of Baxter. Beyond the personal accolade, the award was also proof positive of the power and appeal of his message of values-based leadership.

Harry Kraemer's professional life today is not what he had envisioned. Yet it was only possible because he endured the upheaval that ended a twenty-two-year career at Baxter, including nearly six as CEO. By keeping an open mind and continually engaging in self-reflection, Kraemer has sculpted a life that suits him and his family, allowing him to influence others positively and exhibit his values-based leadership. His philosophy did not make him immune to disappointments, nor did it guarantee success. Rather, he remained grounded in personal principles during his time as CEO, through the transition, and into the next chapter.

When you come out of this cocoon in a
sense, the world is different and it's an
opportunity to explore where it is different.
Where is the growth? Where are the fun and
interesting things happening?

—JACQUES "JAC" NASSER,
FORMER CEO OF FORD MOTOR COMPANY

Chapter Seven

JACQUES "JAC" NASSER
NEW LIFE AFTER A LONG CAREER

When Jacques Nasser graduated from RMIT University in Australia in 1968, two job offers were on the table. After weighing his options, Nasser joined Ford Motor Company as an analyst in the company's operations near Melbourne. For the next thirty-three years, Nasser was a company man, traveling the globe for the automaker: from Australia to Europe, North America, Asia, and South America. He went virtually everywhere the company wanted him to go, helping to develop markets where Ford needed a presence and strengthening or expanding those that were already established.

Looking back, Nasser, who goes by the nickname of Jac, spoke with enthusiasm for each assignment, describing them as fantastic opportunities. Nasser had a great adventure over the years as he created a life he loved by taking on just about any job the company gave to him. In the process, he made a name for himself at Ford, not only as the one to call when opportunity knocked in some far-flung locale, but also for his ability to implement the company's vision. Over the course of his career, he earned praise and recognition, particularly for his work as head of two of the automaker's biggest and most important businesses outside of the United States: Ford Australia and Ford Europe.

Nasser's last assignment with Ford was becoming president and CEO in 1999 following several years as head of its global automotive operations. At the helm of the automaker, Nasser tackled tough issues such as cost-cutting and job reductions, as well as the massive recall of Firestone tires that were linked to safety issues involving the Ford Explorer and other SUVs. He implemented new ways to reach customers via the Internet, and sought to improve the retail and dealership performance while placing an intense focus on the new global product development process—ideas that proved to be a few years ahead of their time. Then, in October 2001, as the auto industry faced challenges due to a souring economy, Nasser was asked to step down.

"I had a strong belief that if you did good things and had fun along the way, then everything else would fall into place. People would be fair and you'd be looked after," Nasser reflected. "It worked for a long time."

Although Nasser had said "yes" to Ford from Argentina to Germany to Mexico to Japan, and many places in between, hearing "no" from the company as his leadership was brought to an end was quite a shock. "It was a huge surprise," he said simply.

For the first time since he graduated from college, Nasser was without a job and a company to call home. In order to move forward, he would need to take some significant time off—something he had not done in all his years at Ford, and certainly not when he was CEO. Only then could he contemplate what he might want to do next.

Going to Work for Ford

Jac Nasser almost started his career elsewhere. Approached by Ford when he was a college student in 1968, he had met with the company several times, but then the automaker disappeared from his job radar. When mining giant BHP approached him, Nasser was ready to accept until he found out that the job would not be in Melbourne, where he was living at the time, but on the eastern coast of Australia. As he pondered what to do, Ford contacted him again. The job that Ford offered was in Melbourne, and Nasser said yes.

Little did the twenty-one-year-old Nasser understand that he had just chosen the company where he would spend the next three decades of his life. The basis of his criteria for choosing Ford over BHP—being able to stay in Melbourne—would soon become irrelevant as he began a globe-hopping career. At the time he accepted the Ford job, however, Nasser had a much more pressing issue: winning over his father, Abdo, who advocated an entrepreneurial path instead of going to work for a company. "My father's view was that if you are really good, why would you need to go to work for someone else? You're better off working for yourself," Nasser recalled. "That's the view he had and still has."

Although father and son took different career paths, they have much in common, including a global perspective. Born in Lebanon, Abdo Nasser grew up mostly in the United States. When World War II broke out, the elder Nasser was visiting Lebanon and had to stay in what was then a French colony governed by the Vichy French. When the Allies arrived, Abdo's English skills landed him a job working for Australian soldiers who were garrisoned in Lebanon. After the war, as he considered where to relocate his family in order to have a better life, Abdo Nasser decided on Australia, settling in the eastern region, where he first worked in an automotive plant and then became an entrepreneur in various fields.

Although Abdo wanted his son to join him in the real estate business, Jac convinced him that taking a job with Ford was a great learning opportunity. In his father's view, Jac would work for Ford for a few years and then do something else. After three or four years working for Ford in Melbourne, however, Jac's choice was to stay with the company, but not in Australia. Instead, in the early 1970s he took a training assignment that brought him first to Europe and then to the United States.

The training assignment in Europe was a real eye-opener for Nasser as to the challenges that Ford faced in diverse, overseas markets. Europe in the 1970s was far different from the unified market of today. "In those days it was seventeen separate countries, each having its own regulations, laws, and safety and emissions standards. Ford's organization reflected that structure. There was a Ford of Britain, a Ford of Germany, a Ford of Spain, a Ford of France. . . . Each one had a unique legal structure and each had developed its own unique products," Nasser explained. This was a far cry from the global perspective that Ford—and Nasser—would later adopt.

After about a year in Europe, Nasser went to work in Dearborn, Michigan, in an entity called Truck Operations, which had been formed when Ford split its business between cars and trucks. For Nasser, the move was a dramatic change, both culturally and climatically. "My family and I left Australia on New Year's Day—summertime in Australia and we had all been down on the beach. I had never been to Michigan before. All I can recall is landing in Detroit and it looked so different to me, all gray and white," Nasser described.

After a year in the United States, Nasser went back to Australia for what turned out to be a relatively short transition. His next assignment was working for the newly formed Ford Asia Pacific, which presented another considerable challenge: separate countries at various stages of economic development. "If you thought Europe was separate back then, the Asia Pacific region was very different: different levels of development, modernization, and industrialization, and different forms of political systems," Nasser added. Despite those complexities, Nasser was willing to go because Ford needed him there.

Ford's vision was to develop an automotive business in Asia by locating production plants in various locations—for example, building engines in Taiwan and transmissions in Indonesia, and operating a stamping facility in the Philippines—and then shipping these engineering-intensive components across borders to supply several markets. The countries, however, all had regulations requiring products and components to be manufactured locally, which ran counter to the Ford plan. "The idea was twenty years before its time," Nasser said.

Despite the operational challenges in Asia, Nasser enthusiastically recalled moving with his family in various Asian countries — and always working in jobs that were fresh and exciting. "No matter how underdeveloped the markets were at that point, you were able to attract the very best people—really smart people who wanted to work for Ford."

From Asia, Nasser went to Venezuela, which was booming in the early 1980s. Ford and its rival General Motors were big players in Venezuela in those days of big cars and cheap gasoline. After three years, Nasser went back to the United States to take on responsibilities for developing manufacturing capability in Mexico through a venture with automaker Mazda. The concept was to combine automotive technology and manufacturing capability with a low-cost location in Mexico to produce products for North America.

When the phone rang next for Nasser, the job opportunity was in Argentina. Following the 1982 Falklands War, a conflict between Argentina and Great Britain over the disputed Falkland Islands, Argentina was transitioning from a military junta to a democracy. The political and business landscape there was vastly different from that in other places Nasser had worked. When Nasser arrived, he was one of the first non-Argentine Ford executives to be sent to the country in order to revitalize operations.

For Nasser, his time in Argentina would be colored by an unusual and dangerous drama: being kidnapped by political extremists. While working in his office at the Ford plant, Nasser was taken hostage by a fringe group that, as he recalled, had some connection with the Peruvian guerilla group Shining Path. Nasser told the story with good humor, downplaying any notion that his life may have been in danger. "They were very nice about it. It was not personal. This was an American company and I was not Argentine. The most important thing to them was the publicity as they accused the

Argentine government of collusion with the imperialistic, capital-istic system."

Despite being taken to an unknown location, Nasser did not feel threatened and remembered his captors as sober and civil. Two days later, they brought him back to his office at the Ford plant with a word of advice and warning. "They said to me, 'The army is coming. We would prefer that you weren't here when that happened.' Then they let me go." A few days later, Nasser—and the Ford operation—were back in business.

In the late 1980s, he was assigned to Brazil, where Ford established a joint venture with Volkswagen. The German auto-maker dominated the Brazilian market, whereas Ford was the leader in the rest of South America. The goal of the joint venture was to combine the expertise and strategic advantages of both automakers to serve the entire Latin American market. "That was a valuable learning experience—so many cultures and different ways of doing things," Nasser remembered. "Think about it: you've got corporate culture, sub-corporate culture, and the culture of all the different Latin American countries. And then you've got two iconic auto companies." In the midst of that unique venture was Nasser, deepening his knowledge and expertise with every experience.

What Nasser remembers best about his early days as a Ford executive working in so many international markets is the value of the opportunities he was given. Still, he didn't pass up a chance to make a joke at his own expense about why he might have been chosen. "There was a common theme with all these assignments. I used to think that when I would get a call asking 'would you be interested in going to this really fascinating market?' they must be calling me first because I was so good at this. Many years later I found out I was most likely the fifteenth person on the list. Usually people in the in the U.S. or Europe didn't want to be too far from the mother ship, although these were interesting jobs in really interesting countries," Nasser observed with a laugh.

Kidding aside, Nasser amassed a global perspective that would become highly prized within Ford as the automaker shifted from tackling separate markets to developing a worldwide strategy. After Brazil, Nasser returned to Australia to run Ford Australia for three years, a homecoming that would become one of his best assignments of all. "Ford Australia started becoming more and more important as part of the growth of Asia," Nasser said. "It was one of the few integrated companies of size inside of Ford. We had unique product development and manufacturing, and were quite vertically integrated because of the size of the market."

Ford Australia also had its share of challenges, which Nasser had to overcome. The book *Customer Centered Growth: Five Proven Strategies for Building Competitive Advantages* described the change in competitive landscape that Ford faced in Australia after that country began to liberalize trade in the 1980s. With more competitors entering the market, Ford's top executives back in the United States wondered whether it made sense to continue product development and manufacturing in Australia. Nasser, however, had a different view.

"After the competitive crisis hit and ominous rumblings from headquarters were heard, Ford Australia president Nasser rallied the organization behind the most compelling overarching purpose possible: survival," authors Richard Whiteley and Diane Hessan wrote. "He clearly described the radical changes it would take to continue existing as more than just a marketing division. He made the painful cuts. And he began developing a positive purpose for Ford Australia in the context of Ford Motor Company's global system."[1]

After his success in strengthening Ford Australia, Nasser was asked to take on another high-profile assignment (and also a favorite): becoming chairman of Ford Europe. "Ford was very strong in Britain, but relatively weak in the rest of Europe," he explained. "We started the transition to having a stronger Ford Europe, with a different focus on the products and establishing low-cost facilities." During Nasser's tenure in Europe, the newly launched Ford Focus was named "European Car of the Year," a top honor in the European automotive industry. In a statement at the time, Nasser observed, "We regard this award as a strong endorsement of the new direction we have chosen to take."[2]

After tackling emerging markets and running large operations such as Ford Europe and Ford Australia, it was time for Nasser to take on the next challenge: going to company headquarters. In the mid-1990s, Nasser went back to Dearborn, this time to run Ford's global product development, where he oversaw a single organization that handled all product planning, research, engineering, and advance engineering for Ford. This was the first time that Ford operated its product development organization on a global basis. "We were going through a period of time when it was important for us as a company to look at the world as one global operation," he explained.

With experience in so many different markets on five continents, Nasser was completely aligned with the company's global perspective.

At Ford Headquarters

As head of the global automotive business in the mid-1990s, Nasser was essentially in charge of 80 percent of Ford operations—everything except the vehicle credit business. In a role akin to being chief operating officer, Nasser reported directly to Alex Trotman, who at the time was chairman and CEO.

In March 1997, Ford announced that Trotman, despite reaching the customary retirement age of sixty-five, would stay on for eighteen months longer, which led to speculation in the media that the extended term would give time to weigh the qualifications of likely successors. It was widely assumed that William Clay Ford Jr., then thirty-nine and the great-grandson of the company founder, would become the chairman. Nasser, then aged forty-nine, was among two executives seen as vying for the CEO post.[3]

In October 1998, Trotman retired. William Ford was given the chairman's position, and Nasser was appointed president and CEO. Although he had been seen as the likely successor to Trotman as CEO, Nasser said the timing was a surprise. "I had thought that I would be in an operating role much longer," he said.

Indeed, Nasser may have benefited from more time in the operating position at Ford headquarters, where he had only been for about three or four years, particularly to build more alliances within the company and to develop closer one-on-one relationships with board members. It is the only thing close to a regret that Nasser expressed when reflecting on thirty-three years with the company.

"I probably should have stayed in Australia longer and in Europe longer. And I probably should have stayed running the global car and truck operations at Ford longer," he said. "You need to be able to change the basic fabric of these large organizations. But when you are in a very fast-paced industry, which the auto industry was and still is, you don't have that luxury. Looking back, though, [having more time in key assignments] would have been one of the areas I would have changed."

But that timing was not to be. When the company offered Nasser the opportunity to become CEO, he said yes.

As a take-charge CEO, Nasser earned his share of praise. Describing his career a few years later, the *New York Times* observed that Nasser "had bold ideas, and many good ones. He . . . was a turnaround expert nicknamed Jac the Knife for his cost cutting."[4]

"The industry was going through a major shift at that time," Nasser described. "That was apparent to most people." For the executive who had readied Ford Australia for an onslaught of competition and who strengthened Ford Europe, he seemed well-positioned to succeed. But for an expatriate executive who had spent the bulk of his career outside the United States, the challenges were significant.

Nasser soon launched a plan to reorganize the company and prepare for the future. As he saw it, the company needed to make strategic changes quickly rather than rest on the laurels of the past. "We had too much capacity and needed to shut down plants. We had too many dealers. We had a technology wave coming at us that would help us in terms of communicating with customers. We had a value chain that wasn't being captured. We had a performance culture in the company in which everyone was rated a high achiever," Nasser said. "There was no direct feedback between compensation, performance, and career development. There was not only a reluctance of individuals [to engage in more meaningful feedback], but management as well. These were uncomfortable discussions to have."

Nasser focused intently on day-to-day operations, including what he saw as critical changes that needed to be made in order to keep Ford a leading competitor. He rolled out a number of initiatives quickly, like a joint venture with Microsoft launched in September 1999 that offered built-to-order vehicles ordered via the Internet. Both companies stressed that the move to allow online customers to configure cars and obtain detailed product information would not displace the traditional car dealer.[5] In January 2000, Nasser announced Ford had signed a deal with Yahoo! to help match up car companies and customers.[6] (What was revolutionary then is standard now, with Web sites such as Yahoo! Autos offering search functions and listings such as "most popular sedans," reviews, and car shopping options.)

Nasser's vision to remake Ford, however, met with resistance. In early 2000, Ford was making strong profits; therefore, changing the status quo did not appeal to many key stakeholders who didn't want any changes to their traditional business model. Nasser admitted that the timing of his plan made it difficult for other parties to swallow. During his tenure (from 1994 to 2001) at the top of Ford

Motor Company—as head of global product development, as president of automotive operations, and then as president and CEO—Ford increased its market capitalization by more than threefold, delivered shareholder returns in the top 25 percent of S&P 500 companies, and posted twelve consecutive quarters of improved earnings. "There is a lesson here that you could see play out later on in the automotive industry," he reflected. "When times are really good, it is the right time to make these changes, but it's also the most difficult time. People will ask, 'If things are so good, why are you trying to fix something that isn't broken?' I think I'm a reasonable communicator and open about things. It was a tough, tough time to be communicating that message."

In hindsight, Nasser acknowledged that he may have taken on too many things too quickly. But on the other hand, he still believes that all the restructuring efforts were necessary. If there is any consolation, it is the conviction that he did what he believed was best for the company and its future and aligned Ford into a stronger position for the long term—particularly compared to its U.S. domestic rivals.

By mid-2000, Nasser was faced with another significant challenge: a safety issue involving certain Ford vehicles, such as Ford Explorers and Ford trucks, due to suspected tire defects. For more than a year, conflict over who was ultimately responsible for the safety defects pitted Ford and Firestone against each other. This contention contrasted with a history of cooperation and connection between the two companies, which had done business together for more than a century and also had ties to the Ford family. (Current Ford CEO William Clay Ford Jr. is the great-grandson of Henry Ford and the great-grandson of Harvey Firestone.)

From the beginning of the tire safety issue, Nasser led a strong offense, acting swiftly and pledging cooperation with the tire industry to develop what was called an "early warning system" to detect tire defects. As he told two House subcommittees in September 2000, "While this is clearly a tire issue and not a vehicle issue, we feel a responsibility to do our best to prevent a situation like this from ever happening again."[7] Despite promises to work together, the tire recall became contentious between Ford and Firestone as the two companies traded accusations over who was at fault.

The tire recall issue, while difficult and costly, was seen by many as a victory for Nasser, whose fast response earned public praise from the company's board. In a statement released by the company in mid-September 2000, company chairman William Ford said, "The management team led by Jac Nasser is doing an outstanding job in a difficult situation. Their focus has been on doing everything possible to get bad tires replaced with good tires and the board fully supports their efforts."[8]

Nasser also gave his team high marks for handling the Firestone issue. "We got the company through the biggest crisis it ever faced with the Firestone situation," he later told *The New York Times*.[9]

For Nasser there would be more challenges ahead. When the U.S. economy soured in 2001, Nasser's task was to reduce costs and reinvigorate sales. In August 2001, Nasser announced that Ford would have to go beyond previously announced job cuts to pare expenses. By that time, Ford had already said it would offer up to 5,000 white-collar employees in North America, or 10 percent of its salaried workforce, a voluntary severance package. Eliminating more jobs and potentially closing a plant were strong possibilities unless the U.S. economy showed signs of rebounding. "This is an initial action," Nasser told reporters at the time. "There will be other actions that we need to take in other areas of the company. . . . We don't see any factor that's going to restore the robustness of the economy. . . . We keep asking ourselves what will it be, what action will happen in the economy that will stimulate confidence in buying again, and we just don't see it."[10]

Nasser's widespread turnaround plans proved to be too much too soon and were particularly challenging for many of the people impacted. Two months later, he was asked to step down. His replacement as CEO was William Clay Ford, who continued to serve as chairman.

The management shakeup, Nasser admitted, caught him off-guard. "I was so focused on the day-to-day and doing what I believed needed to be done, I didn't see it coming." He recalled going into his office after he was told that he was being removed from the CEO position, and wondering what had just happened. As the realization set in, he experienced what he called an eerie feeling: "One minute you are in control and the next minute, literally, you are not," he explained. When his executive team came into his office moments later to express their dismay and support, Nasser's assessment of his situation was blunt but realistic. "I said, 'Look, this is a total shock to me, but it is what it is. And it's clear that you don't want to be somewhere if people have decided that they don't want you.'"

With that, Nasser left behind thirty-three years with Ford Motor Company.

Assessing a Life at Ford

With a distinctive accent, Nasser, now sixty-two, clearly hails from Australia, but Michigan, where Ford is headquartered, is still a home for him, even eight years after his departure from the company. When speaking about his departure from Ford, he did not voice any bitter feelings. "I never got angry. I went farther than I ever thought I'd get," he said. "When I joined Ford, if someone had said to me that I was going to end up a middle-level manager at Ford Australia, I would have said that would be pretty good if I could do that."

Nasser spoke with genuine pride for having been a part of the company at a time it was transforming itself into a global power-house. "Look at what we did in the late 1990s in terms of looking at Ford more as one global entity; changing the product development process so that it was more responsive, flexible and global;

starting to establish more transparency and accountability in terms of organizational performance and leadership development; and . . . growing Ford in places like China, India, Brazil, Turkey, and Russia when it wasn't that obvious that these were ventures that were going to turn out well. When I look back on those decisions that I was part of, and the Ford team, I'm proud of the way the group got together in that period. We were on a roll and it was an exciting period for me and a lot of people who wanted to see the company succeed."

On a more personal level, Nasser can also take pride in his success in a portfolio of assignments that had taken him around the world, with much more diverse international experience than many of his peers in any industry. "I enjoyed all my jobs at Ford—terrific jobs with good, smart people who worked hard. They stretched you in every way. No one can question the integrity of Ford and its people. It was a great experience."

John McArthur, former Dean of the Harvard Business School, observed that Nasser's background and global perspective made him a great asset "especially in a global company." Working in different countries, cultures, and operating environments around the world "must have been an enriching experience for Jac, which also benefited Ford," he added.

What made Nasser successful as an expatriate was his uncanny ability to assimilate quickly. Having grown up speaking English and Arabic, he learned Spanish and Portuguese on the job—and became fluent in both. "The relevancy of that cultural skill, if you want to call it that, was greater then than it is today," Nasser reflected. "Today if you talk to, say, young graduates coming out of a university in Warsaw or in Sao Paulo, their culture is a lot closer now to that of a young graduate coming out of Northwestern University [in suburban Chicago], than it was then."

As Nasser assessed his experiences as the CEO of Ford, he acknowledged that although he had made hundreds of presentations to the board over the years, he knew some individual directors better than others. He did not, however, have a close, one-on-one connection with each of them. He brought to mind the advice he had received from Jack Welch, who was then CEO of General Electric. "Jack said, 'Make sure the board is 100 percent behind you. During certain periods I went through hell, and if I didn't have a board that was 100 percent behind me, I would have been gone.' I didn't pay enough attention to Jack Welch's advice at the time to be quite honest."

Throughout the discussion of his career at Ford, Nasser also downplayed any rivalries or clashes. Instead he spoke with genuine affection for the company and its people—even mentioning that he now owns a Mustang convertible and called himself "too loyal to Ford to flirt with any of those other cars." That same loyalty to Ford had also kept Nasser from considering a career move to another automaker, even though he had opportunities to do so. "Over the years, I had offers from other automotive companies, to sit down and talk with them. I had such a fierce loyalty to Ford at that stage. I still do. I didn't even spend two minutes thinking about career planning or jumping from one company to another," he said. Even now, Nasser would not second-guess his decision to devote virtually his entire career to one company.

When Ford cut its ties to him, however, Nasser had to think about a career outside of the automaker. But first, he would have to make one, key decision: what he did *not* want to do.

Deciding What Not to Do

After leaving Ford, Nasser took off some time to do nothing. This was a common experience among many of the executives with whom we spoke. In Nasser's case, however, that meant going back to Australia to spend time with his father and with his adult children, who came to visit him there. He also pursued things that he hadn't been able to do when he was at Ford, such as reconnecting with friends whom he had known back in school. "It was an opportunity just to relax in a more fluid environment because as an executive your life gets structured in such a way because it has to be—in almost 15-minute intervals. It's an opportunity to unwind without a calendar that drives the pace of your life," Nasser explained. Even today, after going to work in a new capacity, Nasser maintains some flexibility in his schedule.

This need for regular meaningful time off has become the basis of the advice Nasser gives to other CEOs who face similar career upheavals. As he puts it, "Take some time off—real time off. Don't travel down the road and pick up the phone every time it rings. Spend time with family and friends."

Nasser's second decision was not to say yes to the first thing that came along, knowing that a rash decision could be sparked by irrational fear. "You have this thing in the back of your head: the phone is going to stop ringing. No one will call. It isn't real, but it becomes real in your head," he said.

As Nasser considered his options, he decided to start by identifying what he did *not* want to do. One of the first things he ruled out, coming off the experience of being CEO of a firm as complex as Ford Motor Company, was going back immediately to run another public company. The other extreme he decided against was "sitting on the beach and doing nothing for the rest of my life."

With these two options ruled out, Nasser allowed himself to consider any available possibility and talked to as many people as possible about where the opportunities would be in the future. He compared the experience to the young teenager pondering an array of future possibilities, calling it "a healthy process to keep your mind completely open." After a long career with just one company, Nasser was intrigued to see what else might be available to him. "When you come out of this cocoon in a sense, the world is different and it's an opportunity to explore where it is different. Where is the growth? Where are the fun and interesting things happening? Is this [opportunity] realistic to be involved in?" he explained.

In November 2002, a little more than a year after his departure from Ford, Nasser joined One Equity Partners LLC, which was then the private equity business of Bank One Corporation of Chicago, which is now part of JPMorgan Chase. In a statement released at the time, One Equity Partners praised Nasser for his "wealth of global knowledge" and skill in "managing global relationships and complex operations, and in making and integrating bold acquisitions."

For an executive who had spent his entire career with one company, the private equity business, which involves managing multiple investments across numerous companies and industries, was a radical departure—and a welcome change. "What is appealing in private equity is not all your eggs are in one investment basket. In my generation, you just joined an industry and a company and you stayed for a lifetime. . . . I think the obvious advantage of private equity is that you are dealing with, exploring, investing in, and growing many types of businesses in many different industries. It's not only interesting but it's also a natural way to hedge your bets," Nasser said.

"In addition, One Equity Partners is based on backing industrial themes and investing capital behind a business purpose in a truly entrepreneurial spirit," he added. "The other aspect I like about One Equity Partners is that it was founded by a legend in the industry, Dick Cashin [who serves as managing partner], and it is strongly supported by [JPMorgan Chase CEO] Jamie Dimon, who, in my view, is the preeminent global banker. What I admire most in these leaders is their ability to build robust businesses, while keeping an entrepreneurial agility. The lesson here is to be extra careful in choosing the people you want to partner with in your career."

As for the auto industry that Nasser left behind in 2001—but for which he maintains a strong affinity—the financial crisis and severe economic downturn of the past few years appear to have validated many of his efforts, particularly to cut costs, improve efficiency, extend the value chain, and to focus on global products. In 2009, Ford Motor Company could boast that it was the only major U.S. automaker that did not file for bankruptcy; however, it has had to engage in a turnaround effort that included significant debt reduction and efforts to stabilize its U.S. market share. As Ford and other U.S. automakers turned to Washington for bailout help in late 2008, the United Automobile Workers also promised cuts and concessions.

"It's sad in a way, but it also sorted out the weaker players from the stronger players, which in the long term is good," Nasser said. "It was very difficult for a lot of people because they lost careers and lost benefits and livelihoods. But I think from an industry viewpoint, it has given many of these automotive companies—and not just vehicle [manufacturers] but also suppliers and dealers—an opportunity to rebuild an industrial structure that is more sustainable. So I turn the page on the sad and heavy restructuring that has happened over the last year or so with a view that at least now there is a chance for this industry to start with a more level playing field."

Interestingly, Nasser is also turning the page to a new opportunity: one that takes him back to the very beginning of his career with the company that nearly hired him after he graduated college.

A New Role

In 1968, when Nasser weighed two job offers after graduating from RMIT University, Ford Motor Company won out over mining giant BHP. Now, it's BHP's turn to have Nasser in its ranks. In August 2009, following an eighteen-month international search for a chairman, BHP Billiton announced that Nasser would fill that position in early 2010. Until then, Nasser had been a nonexecutive director and a member of the risk and audit committee at BHP since 2006. For Nasser, this is a huge new role as head of the world's largest natural resources company, with products that include petroleum, aluminum, copper, diamonds, iron ore, and coal, and operations worldwide, including Australia, South Africa, North America, and South America. Although he has a new job as chairman of BHP Billiton, Nasser will continue his involvement with the One Equity Partners team.

The man who was not ready to jump back into a CEO role after he left Ford is ready to become chairman of a multinational company, perhaps because of his years on the BHP board or his private equity experience helping to run diverse companies, or perhaps because it is time for the next challenge. Whatever his reasons, when Nasser reflected on his upcoming leadership at BHP, which will involve working in Australia and London and visiting offices and plants worldwide, he explained that what appealed to him about the company were the same factors that had made Ford so attractive back in the 1960s: "a global company; products that are important for the growth of the developed and developing world; a business that is a mix of everything from technology to research and development, and working with smart, dedicated people."

When he takes over as chairman of BHP, Nasser will be back more often in Australia where his father, now ninety-eight, still lives. When asked who has influenced his leadership more than any other person, Nasser quickly credited his father. Beyond being a role model for successfully relocating to different countries and cultures, Abdo Nasser has had a big impact on his son's approach to life and business. "He's just an incredible, very optimistic person," Nasser said of his father. "He starts with, 'Let's decide what we want to do and let's decide how we are going to do it. Let's sit down together and work through this.' With him, it's always the glass being half-full or even a full glass. That doesn't mean that he's unrealistic about things. He always has a level of optimism and confidence I wish I could have had more often in my career—an unwavering level of confidence and a belief that things will work out in the long term if you work at them."

Nasser also observed that his father values persistence and believes that there are no such things as barriers except the obstacles that one places on oneself. Looking over his thirty-three-year career at Ford and what has followed with success at One Equity Partners, Nasser can take pride in his track record at scaling barriers, particularly early on when he never knew for sure in what part of the world he'd be working next or what challenge would meet him in a particular marketplace.

Taking on a new role in a dynamic, global industry seems particularly fitting for Nasser after a long career at Ford and successful years in private equity. One also imagines that it must be a source of pride for both father and son that, as chairman of BHP Billiton, Nasser is assuming what *The Australian* called "corporate Australia's most prestigious role."[11] Jac Nasser has found an expanded corporate life for himself—one for which he appears to be uniquely positioned and qualified. "Talk about back to the future—I am now back to BHP Billiton as chairman, a journey that started almost forty years ago, while at the same time heeding my father's entrepreneurial advice and example by continuing my role with JPMorgan's One Equity's Partners," Nasser observed.

And his father is happy his son is coming home.

No matter how bleak and how terrible things look, or whatever the perceptions are, there is life after what you experience or what you have gone through. It is not necessarily apparent at that period of time.

—DURK JAGER, FORMER CHAIRMAN AND CEO,
PROCTER & GAMBLE COMPANY

Chapter Eight

DURK JAGER
PEACE OF MIND AND
WALKING AWAY

When Durk Jager looks back over his thirty-year career with Procter & Gamble (P&G) he sees a professional time line that has been marked at various points by highs and lows: jobs he enjoyed and those that were difficult, notable successes and some defeats. Overall, though, he is satisfied with what he has achieved and speaks with pride for having been part of an organization he deeply admires. Jager has few regrets as he recounts his three decades at the global consumer products giant that sells a variety of products under iconic brands such as Tide laundry detergent, Crest toothpaste, and Pampers diapers.

Accepting who he is and what he was able to accomplish over the years allowed Jager to gain perspective and peace of mind after he resigned as CEO. After leaving his post, he and his wife left Ohio, where P&G is headquartered, and drove down to their vacation home in Alabama. Somewhere along the way, Jager, who was then fifty-six, decided it was time to rethink his professional life. Being a CEO after a hard-driving, globe-trotting career no longer held an appeal. Life changed. Priorities shifted. It was time for something else: serving on boards, being a consultant, devoting time to favorite charities, and contemplating what matters the most, especially spending time with his family. Speaking in his pleasant Dutch accent, Jager succinctly summarized the shift in his outlook and thinking by saying, "I have become much more philosophical."

Jager concluded that there is no need to replicate what has already been done. He has moved on, which for him has meant doing exactly that: going on to something else where he can contribute his knowledge, expertise, and wisdom. Although he never went back to the corporate world as an executive, Jager has hardly been idle since he left P&G. His desire to stay intellectually stimulated and to give back are strong motivators. He has plans for the future, albeit with a narrower scope than in the past. Jager is still an innovator, a role that has clearly been his first love over a long career that began back in Europe when he was in his twenties.

Today, at the age of sixty-six, Jager is in the emeritus stage of his professional life, from which he can review the entire course of his career, including steady promotions, being groomed for corporate leadership, and plans that worked out and some that did not. With one strong statement he voiced his acceptance of it all, including what happened during his time as CEO, when the company faced challenges to reinvent itself and his turnaround plans proved to be too much, too fast: "I have done my best." That knowledge has allowed Jager to move beyond disappointment and to embrace his success.

Joining P&G

It's no surprise that Durk Jager would become an innovator, given his interest early on in how things work. He grew up in a small town in the Netherlands, where his father was a local banker, and then went to a technical university to study aeronautics, but soon decided that this particular field did not suit him. "I figured out pretty quickly that with planes there were only two possibilities: either they flew or they didn't fly. I needed a whole gray area in between," he recalled.

Married in his early twenties, Jager worked while he attended Erasmus University in Rotterdam to receive an advanced degree in business. By the time he graduated at age twenty-seven, it was the 1970s and Jager was still living in the Netherlands, which seemed too small and with limited possibilities. When he saw an advertisement for open positions at P&G, he applied for a job there and joined the company as a sales trainee in Brussels, where its European operations were based. He would finally have his chance to explore the "gray area" between success and failure, which in consumer products came down to a company's ability to test ideas, understand consumer perceptions, communicate value, and launch and build brands.

Over the next few years, Jager was trained by P&G in Europe and the United States, gaining a strong foundation in how the company did business, which still influences him today. "I learned a lot. I saw the system and how people operated. I respected many of the beliefs that the company had. They were deeply ingrained in me. I still believe in them," Jager said. In the late 1970s, he brought those lessons with him when he returned to Holland, where he was a group manager in P&G's advertising unit. "We felt that brands were based on advertising, not on coupons and promotions," he added.

Another one of the big lessons Jager learned early in his career was summarized by a powerful axiom: We invest in success and not in failure. "At P&G, we exploited the positive; we put money into advertising in areas that already worked," he said. "If it works, invest more. In business where continual survival is the key objective, it was a recipe for success."

In the years to come, P&G would invest in Jager's success as well, moving him from job to job, region to region, from Europe to Asia to North America. As his career unfolded, he gathered experiences and lessons, applying what proved to be valuable and rethinking what did not produce the desired results. As an innovator he was not afraid to question, to test, and to try something new.

By the 1980s, Jager had moved with P&G to Austria, where he eventually became the head of the operation. This was the perfect assignment, the ideal place as he saw it: a big enough market to make an impact, but just far enough away from P&G's European business center in Brussels to enjoy some autonomy. "For a couple of years I was very happy. I remember that I told my boss that I would want to stay there forever," Jager recalled. "The very next day, he told me I was being sent to Japan."

Japan was a difficult assignment that lasted from 1982 through 1988. Personally, it was a challenge for Jager and his family to be so far from home and in the midst of an unfamiliar culture. The best way to deal with the separation from extended family and what was familiar was to return to the Netherlands for visits every few months. From a business perspective, Japan was a challenging market in which to gain consumer loyalty, with P&G "losing $1 for every $1 of sales" it made there, Jager explained. The problem was a lack of acceptance of American-designed products by Japanese consumers. Redesigning these products for the local market, however, required convincing the research and development (R&D) department back in the United States.

Jager also had to wrestle with how to design and launch the most effective consumer messages for the Japanese market, including whether to work with the overseas offices of large U.S. agencies or to go with Japanese firms. Jager decided the best approach was with Japanese agencies that knew the market very well, even though communication was often difficult. Despite all the challenges, Jager described his job in Japan as a learning experience—not as a hardship to endure. "We gained incredible insights: what people react to, what was culturally appropriate," he said. Jager's experiences in Japan offer an insight into his approach: If there is a problem, it must be identified and solved; there is no hoping it will change or wishing it could be another way.

The most important learning Jager extracted from his experience in Japan was that P&G's usual approach of mimicking U.S.

product rollouts in international markets did not always work. What appealed to consumers in one country did not necessarily draw those in another. Rather than replicating overseas the product marketing strategies and job functions that worked in the United States, a better approach was to tailor strategies to local markets. These ideas about appealing to customers and meeting their needs would surface later on when Jager was a top leader at P&G helping the company to improve its global competitive strategy.

After Japan, Jager's next opportunity was to run the entire Far East operation, a job he held for about a year and a half in the late 1980s. At the time, P&G was growing through product innovation, which often drew upon new technologies that could be married with existing brands, such as suspended silicones to improve shampoos and conditioners in P&G's Pantene brand. The acquisition earlier in 1985 of Richardson-Vicks, maker of Vicks cough drops, also allowed new products such as cold medicine to be launched under the well-known Vicks brand. As valuable as these innovations and acquisitions were to P&G, most did not result in new brands for the company—exactly what P&G would need to generate long-term, sustained growth.

In the late 1980s, as Jager was preparing to return to the United States, he received a powerful lesson—which would have a lasting impression on him—about the value of questioning the status quo. The occasion was a retirement dinner for a long-time executive. In his farewell speech, the executive recalled how impressed he had been with various people he had worked with over his thirty-year career, with the roles they played in the community and in industry associations. Then the executive voiced an observation that made an "incredible impression," as Jager recalled it. "He said, 'I wonder why this company isn't doing better? You take this collection [of people, brands, and businesses] and all the capabilities that we have, and yet our results are not what they should be.' This was the first time I heard criticism of the company from a very senior guy who was about to retire."

At that moment, Jager learned that it really was not possible to evaluate whether certain practices had contributed to growth or inadvertently impeded it unless people were willing to speak up about unrealized potential in a company that had many strengths— from well-known brands to highly capable and talented people. In the years to come, perhaps recalling the words of that retiring executive, Jager would wonder many of the same things: Why wasn't the company doing better? His thinking would become part of his drive to reduce unnecessary complexity, improve innovation, and revitalize growth.

In 1989, when the company was shuffling its top management, Jager was promoted to a high-ranking leadership role in the United States. As candidates were picked and groomed, it became clear that Jager had captured the company's attention as a possible contender in the succession race. John Smale resigned as chairman and CEO, effective January 1990. He was succeeded by Edwin Artzt, whom Jager had worked with in international operations. When Artzt became CEO, John Pepper was selected to run the international business. Jager, meanwhile, was one of two leaders running the entire U.S. business. In June 1991, when P&G shifted executives again, Jager, then forty-eight and an executive vice president, took charge of all U.S. products, including packaged soap; cleaning, health care, and beauty products; paper; food; and beverage operations. He reported directly to Artzt.

In the early 1990s, poor economic conditions presented U.S. operations a challenge. As *BusinessWeek* described in November 1993, "In the past three years, cash-strapped buyers have cut back on purchases or traded down to lower-priced products, shunning P&G's premium brands. In diapers, the company's market share is under 40 percent—up a bit in recent months but far below its nearly 50 percent share in the late 1980s. Now, though, P&G is showing signs that its strategy of slicing prices and promotions while spewing out new products is giving it a new lease on its markets."[1]

Artzt was credited with a companywide restructuring that closed one-fifth of P&G's factories and reduced the workforce by 12 percent. Then in July 1995, after forty-one years with the company, Artz turned sixty-five and stepped down as chairman and CEO. The succession plan not only named Artz's replacement but also indicated the next likely move for Jager as he was further groomed for leadership.

Artz's successor was John E. Pepper, then aged fifty-six, described in the media as a "gentlemanly consensus-builder" and a thirty-two-year veteran of P&G. In the same move, P&G's board also signaled the heir apparent to Pepper: Jager. The *New York Times* called Jager, who was in the position of president and chief operating officer, "a highly competitive, 51-year-old strategist with an impatient streak." The *Times* quoted analysts on Pepper's and Jager's differing styles, labeling Pepper as the "ambassador of good will" and Jager as "more in line with [former CEO] Ed Artzt, a real results-oriented executive."[2]

Looking back, Jager acknowledged that their differing styles did make for a challenging operating dynamic, as did the fact that there was no clear separation of duties between him as president and chief operating officer and Pepper as CEO and chairman. "My style and his style in business and people management were quite the opposite," Jager said. "But we were colleagues. We made it work."

The company continued facing difficulties in the marketplace. As Jager described, there was too much complexity in P&G's brands that had been extended with off-shoot products, which resulted in many product variations that were not clearly differentiated. "Tide plus Downey [fabric softener]—that was our perception of innovation in those days, instead of introducing a new Tide or a new Downey, or creating new products," he explained. "The consumer couldn't figure out the choices. The satisfaction with products became poorer and poorer."

As Jager focused on efforts to improve the design, testing, and launch of products into the marketplace, he saw a vital need for

P&G to return to its roots of innovation. Invention and new product development were truly the legacy of the company, which dated back to a partnership between William Procter and James Gamble in 1837. In the 1870s, one of its early flagship products, Ivory Soap, was marketed nationally and transformed the company into a manufacturer of branded goods for consumers.[3]

When Pepper retired, Jager took over as CEO in January 1999, and became chairman in September of that year. His mission was to recapture the company's legacy by introducing all-new brands and product lines—something that he said had not been done at P&G throughout the entire 1990s. His other marching orders, as Jager called them, were to increase profit margins and improve financial performance, which also underscored the importance of new brands to capture consumer interest and spending.

To promote research and development, $250 million was set aside, Jager recalled. "Unless you create new brands, the oxygen goes out of the thing. You also lose brands over time. Some have outlived their time. You have to replenish that funnel."

Jager was also not afraid to shake up what was widely described as P&G's "conformist culture." His plans were ambitious and his pace was swift, as outlined by what was unveiled in 1999 as Organization 2005: a six-year, $1.9 billion effort to rapidly restructure the company through changes in organizational structure, work processes, and culture, all geared at encouraging—and accelerating—innovation. Jager had been a key player in developing plans for Organization 2005 while he was president and chief operating officer. As CEO, he was expected to use the extensive restructuring program called for under Organization 2005 to launch new blockbuster brands rather than relying on incremental improvements in existing products. Looking back, Jager reflected on the need to jumpstart creativity at P&G, in order to reinvigorate the company with a new sense of urgency and competitiveness. "We felt our operations had become so slow. That was demonstrated and illustrated by a lack of real product innovation. We had to change the structure," he said.

As Jager took over as CEO, the press assessed the difficulties that he faced, which amounted to nothing less than redoing how a 160-year-old company operated. "To succeed, Jager must re-engineer P&G's formidable corporate culture," *Marketing Week* observed. "Over the years, P&G has always fought hard to launch new products with a tangible point of difference. But in mature First World markets, product superiority is becoming ever more tricky to achieve and sustain. Somehow, Jager has to find ways of stimulating innovation and escorting the new product to market a lot more rapidly—an infinitely more difficult task than introducing the new management system."[4]

The task given Jager was a weighty one. P&G's sales had been almost stagnant in the 1990s, although by late 1998 they were showing signs of picking up. It would be up to Jager to double sales by 2006—a very ambitious goal. "He plans to do so by introducing a seven-division global category management system and ruthlessly pruning top-heavy management at the same time. That should certainly please the shareholders and speed decision making. But it will be nowhere near enough," *Marketing Week* added.[5]

Jager sought to revitalize P&G's well-entrenched corporate culture, in which the *modus operandi* involved layers of procedures for designing, evaluating, and testing products. This process was too slow for a demanding and highly competitive marketplace, Jager believed. Streamlining the processes from idea to product development to product in consumer hands was the only way to reinvigorate growth.

As part of Jager's drive for new growth, one of the first big successes was Swiffer, a floor-cleaning device that uses an electrostatic disposable sheet to trap dust and dirt, which was introduced while Jager was still president and COO. Swiffer found broad acceptance as a leading product in 1999, his first year as CEO. "We were extremely fast rolling it out. We eventually made a whole line from that product that came later," Jager said.

A November 1999 feature in the Cincinnati Enquirer hailed the success of Swiffer, which at the time was already facing competition from nearly identical products from other companies. One of P&G's fastest-selling new products ever, Swiffer was expected to top $300 million in retail sales the first year. In the article, a spokesman for retailer Kroger Co. called it "the hit of 1999 in the household cleaning category." The Enquirer quoted Laura King, brand manager for Swiffer, who credited direct intervention from Jager to keep Swiffer on track for launching. As the newspaper reported, "'Durk was pushing for the new culture,' King said of Jager's unusual intrusion into what had been P&G's standard product development process—a labyrinth it is trying furiously to change."[6]

The article also noted that P&G had accelerated its plans to take Swiffer global—moving at a pace that cut the time to market in half. Rather than rest on the laurels of its Swiffer success, P&G was already testing new products. As King summarized in the newspaper article, "Durk's mantra is 'make a little, sell a little and learn a lot' . . . He's changing this company from conservative to risk-taking. It's empowering. It allows people who understand consumers best to make decisions."[7]

In addition to streamlining P&G's process of getting products to market with much greater speed, Jager also tackled the company's geographic structure, which was burdened with layers of general managers and category managers in individual countries and broader regions. "A geographic structure doesn't make any sense," Jager said. Instead of focusing on organizing the company in separate countries and regions, he put in place global business units to manage the strategic planning and launching of products in the United States and abroad.

"All the consumer cares about is if she gets a better or safer detergent. We started out with what can we do for the consumers in a better and more efficient way, and then we looked at the various activities in the company," Jager summarized.

Jager's emphasis on innovation together with his new global business unit structure were credited with the launching of new successful products besides Swiffer, including Febreze, a fabric deodorizer, and Dryel, a home dry-cleaning product. As a Harvard Business School case study noted, "To drive his vision, Jager frequently scrutinized P&G's R&D portfolio and personally stewarded new technologies through the pipeline that he felt were promising."

The results of the efforts surfaced quickly. Quarterly earnings in October 1999, the first quarter of fiscal 1999–2000, showed sales up 5 percent, compared with 2.6 percent annual revenue growth for the previous two years. Quarterly earnings excluding restructuring costs increased by 10 percent—described as "quite respectable for the first full quarter of any restructuring program."[8]

Not all of Jager's ideas worked, or at least didn't come to fruition during his tenure as CEO. For example, his offer to acquire Gillette Company, which made razors and batteries, was rebuffed. Then five years later, in 2005, his successor brought the deal together in a $57 billion acquisition. Jager had also pursued acquisitions of pharmaceutical companies Warner-Lambert and American Home Products, but media leaks and speculation about a possible deal soured the opportunity.

When it came to making changes internally at P&G, Jager said many in the company shared his view and some wanted to be more aggressive. As he saw it, there was a real desire at P&G to do things differently. However, the engrained and entrenched culture that developed and had been reinforced over decades did result in real resistance. In hindsight, Jager conceded that his plans may have been too much to tackle all at once, although there was a benefit to implementing them everywhere at the same time. "I was between a rock and a hard place," he observed. "So I wish [in hindsight] that I had been a little more careful and moved in smaller steps."

Early 2000 brought a bubble in the market as stocks were at lofty levels. The run-up in the stock market pushed P&G to a price-to-earnings ratio (a benchmark of how much of a price premium is in a stock) of 37, which was uncommonly high for a consumer goods company. It also proved to be a precarious perch for P&G. "It was a period of time when something very little going wrong could hurt you in a tremendous way," Jager said.

On March 7, 2000, P&G, citing higher raw material costs and price pressure, announced an earnings warning: specifically that earnings per share for the quarter ending March 31, 2000, would be 64 to 65 cents, compared with analysts' estimates of around 78 cents. Jager told CNN in an interview, "We're obviously very disappointed with what happened. We believe this is a temporary setback—the fundamentals of our business are sound." The stock market, however, was unforgiving. P&G's shares fell sharply: closing the day down $25.9375 at $61.50 a share—and accounting for about 142 points of a steep 374-point drop in the Dow Jones Industrial Average.[9]

In discussions with analysts at the time, Jager pointed out the company's commitment to getting product innovations to market faster and promised a closer focus on P&G basics—"hardnosed cost management as well as accelerating sales growth." The company also boasted fifty new products in the pipeline.[10]

Yet in an uncertain and volatile environment, such promises would not be enough to overcome doubts that were being cast on Jager's plans. Three months later, he would be out of a job.

A Quick Exit

For Jager, the departure happened before he had much time to contemplate it. With the stock price under pressure (which also hurt the value of stock options held by company executives) rumblings began to surface about whether Jager's ambitious reorganization would produce the desired results. Eventually, Jager was confronted by a board member who conveyed, somewhat indirectly, that there was a lack of support for his leadership.

What was said to Jager could only lead to one conclusion: his time as CEO was over after only seventeen months. "I walked out. That was it. I never talked to the board," Jager said of his resignation. "I left an hour later, after thirty years."

When Jager talked about the board member's lack of directness, it was the only time in our conversation that he came close to expressing any criticism of how his departure was handled. "Nobody walked in my office and said, 'Hey Durk, explain what this is. What's happening?'" Jager said. "I thought it was cowardly. If there is a struggle, I would come in and say, 'How would you like to solve it?' That's the normal way you operate."

Media reports on his departure credited Jager for his attempts to revitalized P&G. "Under Mr. Jager . . . the company tried to bolster a mediocre growth rate by developing products more quickly, eschewing the many-layered approval processes and market tests for which the conservative company was famous," the *New York Times* noted. "Mr. Jager also moved many managers to new jobs to shake up a corporate culture in which employees are called Proctoids because of their efficiency and obedience."[11] However, the consensus among critics was that the reorganization plan had been too broad-based and too aggressive.

Looking back, Jager stoically accepted the circumstances that put an end to his long career at the company. "I can fully understand that it is a meritocracy. If you fail, whether it's your fault or not, there are consequences," he said.

What bothered Jager deeply was the fact that a fall in the share price had hurt the long-term savings and net worth of many people who worked for the company and participated in P&G's employee stock ownership plan (ESOP). "Their fortunes were tied to the company. I felt deeply responsible," he added.

Jager, who had the shortest tenure as CEO of any executive in P&G's history, also was symbolic of the times. As *Fortune* magazine noted, Jager's swift departure was "sounding awfully familiar," adding that there had been executive-suite turnover at other companies such as Coca-Cola, Mattel, Campbell Soup, and Xerox around the same time. "Jager's departure shows, if anybody still wondered, that you don't get much time to prove yourself anymore, and if you stumble at one of these brand behemoths, you may not even have a chance to get up."[12]

When Jager got up again, it was on his own terms. "I had always dreamed that at fifty-five, fifty-six, or fifty-seven I would do something else," he recalled. "There was no sense trying to get a second shot at being a CEO. I got a couple of offers, but there was no real inclination to do that." Another motivation to stay off the corporate career track was the desire to focus more on his family, particularly after two family members faced serious health issues from which they have recovered.

"Our attention and our priorities changed," Jager said. After three decades of being a results-oriented executive, Jager's focus shifted to home and the well-being of his family. This created a change in his life, which, in turn, influenced his outlook. He became more reflective, a trait that he articulates clearly today. "When you get older, you become longer-term in your perspective, which is counterintuitive," Jager said. "But you do think long-term and focus on those things that are most important."

To take a longer-term view of one's life and accomplishments, instead of overemphasizing a single event of success or failure, requires a healthy sense of self-esteem and a well-balanced definition of who a person is, observed Dr. Leonard Elkun, a practicing psychiatrist in Chicago who has worked in issues related to retirement and aging. "If a person can really appreciate himself for the efforts he has put forth in whatever endeavor, whether it is running a Fortune 500 company or painting the back fence, then if something negative occurs, it will not knock him off the perch of feeling good about himself," Elkun added. "The critical issue is self-esteem maintenance."

If a person does not have a strong and balanced sense of self-esteem, the desire for validation becomes a self-perpetuating cycle of needing constant external reinforcement and admiration. This attitude can become problematic with people who can only feel good about themselves if they meet or exceed the high expectations they set for themselves, Elkun explained. Instead of feeling satisfied if certain goals are achieved, they only feel relief from not having failed to achieve these goals. "Individuals who are married to outcome are perpetually disappointed," Elkun added. "This is particularly pertinent to CEOs who will have achieved an enormous amount, but never feel satisfied or content because the personal goals they set for themselves are rarely achievable."

In his conversation with us, it was apparent that Jager has realized that balance between who he is and what he has achieved. This has allowed him to retain an appreciation for his career at P&G, a company he admires enormously and cares about deeply to this day, even though his term as CEO ended prematurely. He can look back on his career with few regrets because he is grounded in the entirety of what he contributed to the company over a long career, not just a final challenging few months.

Asked what he might have done differently, now with the benefit of hindsight, Jager admitted that he has heard observations since his departure from P&G that if "I had done XYZ I might still be there, although I would have retired by now." Such musing is not valuable, Jager added, for the simple fact that it is impossible to change the past.

Second guessing one's decisions and actions are even less helpful when a person believes that he or she had done the right things based upon what was known at the time and the circumstances he or she faced. The only benefit in engaging in such thinking, Jager added, is to acknowledge the experience of what happened and take it in as a lesson. "Experiences are collectively a big jigsaw puzzle," he said. "Any decision that you make or step you are considering is the result of the decisions that came before it."

For Jager, the longer he stayed off the corporate track, the more appealing his new life became. After running P&G, he had no burning desire to do it all again, especially given the grueling demands on one's time and energy. "For ten years I had been flying to Asia and Europe. Once you are out of that, you don't respond extremely well to it," he said. But he did not want to be idle. Jager has a desire to stay involved, which continues to this day.

Eventually, Jager joined the boards of two companies in the Netherlands, where he had not been active in business for decades. One was the Dutch national telecommunications company, Royal KPN, after it was privatized. The other was Royal Wessanen, a premium food company catering to European and North American consumers. He also serves on the board of Chiquita Brands. Previously, he was on the board of Kodak, starting in 1998 when he was president of P&G. Discussing his board assignments past and current, Jager called them interesting and often complex. His experience as CEO of a global operation and his perspective as an executive who understands the need to strategize for the future and not just the short-term—a lesson he learned first-hand at P&G—makes Jager a valuable board member.

Lessons from P&G

Although Jager left P&G in 2000, the company has hardly left him. He remains strongly influenced by many of the values and disciplines at the firm, including its famous "one-page memo." (P&G has informally enforced a long-time policy that virtually every communication has to fit on one page, which encourages conciseness.)

Jager learned a big lesson from his years at P&G: the need for leaders to foster ideas without letting the bureaucracy that often exists in large corporations stifle them. "Innovation doesn't happen in a team. You can make your execution better in a group. But an individual wrestles with an idea and tests it," Jager said.

Another lesson, which Jager learned at P&G and that was later reinforced at Kodak where he was a board member, was the need to strike the necessary balance between valuing brands and not being afraid to dismantle them when their time has come to an end. In companies where brands enjoy an extraordinarily high market share for a period of time, such thinking is cutting-edge, if not downright heretical. But no product or brand remains unchallenged by competitors. If a company isn't committed to introducing new products—including ones that might challenge its brand stalwarts—its competitors will. "You have to learn that unless you are willing to destroy them [long-term brands and products], someone else is going to do it for you," Jager said.

Jager gave the example of Spic and Span, a powdered cleaning product, that when he joined the company had about a 90 percent market share. (The name of the product even worked its way into everyday language as an adjective for clean.) Rather than branch out and build on that success, the company never looked at such variations as liquid cleaners until it was too late. "The definition of your market determines your success," he said. "You need to look at your market every time you have a chance."

A corollary lesson Jager learned is that when a new product or brand is launched, there is sometimes a temptation to view the market too narrowly, rather than seeing the full potential. "A traditional belief has been to define your market narrowly because then you are better focused, which is B.S. You have to think about the market in the biggest sense, even though some areas may not be addressable," Jager added. Companies that fail to learn that lesson may soon be reminded of it when their competitors surpass them.

As Jager looked back on his career, he also assessed his own style of managing and communicating, which he described as direct and decisive—a trait he said he shared with his father. "There are two contrasting styles. There is a group of people who are very comfortable postponing every decision to get more advice," he observed. "I have been the opposite. After I have done the due diligence, then I make the decision and go on to the next one, which is often more important than the previous one."

Although Jager believes consensus and compromise are often needed, they cannot override individual responsibility. "I hate team-itis, when every governance structure in a company is called a team," Jager said.

Jager's views were bound to ruffle some feathers, particularly in a large company with an entrenched way of operating. Yet Jager wouldn't change anything: not himself and his management style, and certainly not the plans he implemented, which he deeply believed were needed for the good of the company. In fact, Jager would not have altered the three decades he spent with P&G, where colleagues and corporate leaders had a profound influence on him. "I never thought about leaving, although I got a number of opportunities. I was very comfortable with the style and situation," he said.

Like so many other CEOs interviewed, Jager also spoke with gratitude and, thinking back on where and when he started, even with some surprise at the level to which he had risen at the company. "I never thought I would get to where I did," he said. "With a little luck, I thought maybe I would be a country manager for the Netherlands. I am reasonably proud. I lived in a way that I wanted to live as a principled person. I worked hard and didn't play the convenient role. I am happy that I have been in some situations in which I have been able to demonstrate that. That is what life is—not just in business but also in your personal life. You work hard and do the best you can, and take charge of the responsibilities given to you."

Jager learned a final lesson when he departed, which he not only took to heart but also shares with others who may be going through similar experiences. The advice came from one of the few board members who reached out to Jager after he left P&G. In a letter to Jager the director wrote, "There is life after Procter."

Contemplating those words anew, Jager reflected on the wisdom they contain, especially in the midst of any upset: personal or professional. In time comes a new perspective on what may have felt devastating or looked hopeless. "No matter how bleak and how terrible things look, or whatever the perceptions are, there is life after what you experience or what you have gone through," he shared. "It is not necessarily apparent at that period of time."

What helps, Jager added, is to consider the challenges that others have faced, which provides perspective and even inspiration that setbacks can be overcome and success realized or regained. "You look at what other people have faced, which often is imminently more difficult."

Jager has the consolation of knowing in his heart that he did the best he could, and he accepts the inevitable fact that some things do not work out as planned. One's character, however, is defined and tested under such circumstances, when difficulties arise and disappointments are faced. With candor and class, Jager accepted what happened, never sought to blame others, and through it all voiced his appreciation for the company that gave him an incredible career. He has, indeed, found life—and peace—after Procter.

If you are all wrapped up in a company, if that is the only thing that means something to you, it's a flaw. What about your family and your children, your health, and your country?

—JAMIE DIMON, CHAIRMAN AND CEO OF JPMORGAN CHASE, FORMER PRESIDENT OF CITIGROUP

Chapter Nine

JAMIE DIMON
THE ULTIMATE COMEBACK

I n the corporate world, Jamie Dimon is the ultimate comeback story, which over the years has taken on nearly legendary proportions. The details are well known: Working with long-time boss Sanford "Sandy" Weill, Dimon rose through the ranks of predecessor firms that eventually became Citigroup. Although the inner circle of Citigroup management became crowded with several executives, Dimon held the title of president and, as the presumed heir apparent to Weill, was thought to be the person most likely one day to run what was then the world's largest financial services company.

Then one Sunday afternoon in November 1998, Dimon was called into a meeting with Weill and John Reed, who as co-CEOs ran Citigroup, and was fired. Eighteen months later, in March 2000, Dimon reemerged as chairman and CEO of Chicago-based Bank One, a regional bank in need of a turnaround. By 2004 Dimon was back in New York after Bank One was purchased by JPMorgan Chase. In 2006, Dimon became chairman and CEO of JPMorgan. Today he is widely regarded as the leading statesman and operating executive in the financial services industry and is at the helm of one of the strongest institutions to have weathered the financial crisis of 2007–2008.

Dimon's story has all the elements of a classic comeback. After being fired from a lofty position at the leading company in the industry at the time, he is now in a significantly broader and more impactful role. The company he leads today is also viewed as stronger, and larger in terms of market capitalization, than the firm from which he was forced to resign. But to see Jamie Dimon's story only as a triumphant rise after a public fall is to miss the more important and deeper lessons of what has guided his journey.

In a recent interview, Dimon reflected back on being fired from Citigroup at the age of forty-two. Although the experience caused him emotional upset, it did not undermine his sense of self. As his wife, Judy Dimon, put it, "I never defined Jamie by his job, and he never defined himself by his job." As a result, throughout the ordeal Dimon was sustained by the fundamental belief, which he often stated, that his "net worth, not [his] self worth" was impacted when he was fired from Citigroup.

Although he was too young to sit on the sidelines after this career disappointment, Dimon was in no rush to make a move. Rather than jump at one of the potential opportunities that came along, Dimon vowed not to start his job search in earnest for at least six months. Only then did he "try on" various opportunities until he found the one that fit not only in the context of his career, but also with regard to what would be best for his wife and their three young daughters.

With unwavering support from those closest to him, and with a strong sense of who he is versus what he does, Dimon chose the best opportunity available from which to relaunch his career—thereby putting himself in a position that would take him far beyond his prior accomplishments.

Focused on Success

James "Jamie" Dimon was born in March 1956 in Queens, New York, and spent his early formative years there, before later moving with his family to an apartment on Park Avenue in Manhattan. From an early age, he had his sights on success and developed a good bit of confidence. As his father, Ted, told *BusinessWeek* in

1996, he once asked Dimon and his two brothers what they wanted to be when they grew up. Peter, the oldest brother, said a physicist. Ted, Jamie's twin brother, didn't have his mind made up yet. Jamie, however, voiced big plans: "He wanted to run something . . . ," his father recalled.[1]

Luckily for Dimon, he got a head start in a business that would, indeed, make him very successful: financial services. His father, Ted, has been a stockbroker for almost sixty years. His grandfather, who emigrated from Greece to the United States in 1919 and changed the family name from Papademetriou to Dimon, had also been a stockbroker. While he was in college in the 1970s, Dimon worked summers for his father and grandfather, which gave him a taste of the brokerage business. At the time, his father worked for a brokerage firm (which would later become Shearson) run by Sandy Weill, and was friendly with him. Through this connection, Dimon met Weill, who would later become his boss and who would have the strongest influence over his early career.

After graduating summa cum laude from Tufts University in 1978, Dimon took a job with Management Analysis Center, a consulting firm in Boston. Two years later, he enrolled in Harvard Business School, where Dimon eschewed the preppy, button-down look of his peers and instead wore blue jeans, T-shirts, and a leather jacket. His choice of apparel aside, Dimon stood out for other reasons, including becoming a Baker Scholar, a distinction given to MBA students who graduate with honors. While at Harvard he met Judy Kent, a fellow student, and the two married in 1983.

In the early 1980s, Wall Street drew young talent like the proverbial magnet, and Dimon was no exception. He entertained job offers from the leading firms, including Goldman Sachs, Morgan Stanley, and Lehman Brothers. As he weighed the opportunities presented to him, Dimon consulted with Weill. Instead of getting advice on which Wall Street firm to join, Weill offered Dimon an entirely different plan: come to work for him at American Express. At the time, American Express had just bought

Weill's brokerage firm, Shearson, and Weill had been named president. Dimon was hired to be his assistant.

For Dimon, the decision to go to work for Weill could not have been an easy one since a job at an investment bank such as Goldman Sachs would have paid him 60 percent more than the position at American Express. In the end, Dimon went to work for Weill because, as he described in a speech at Northwestern University in 2004, "my goal in life was not to be a partner in an investment bank, and frankly it wasn't money. It was to build something, whatever that meant. . . . "[2] As his career progressed, Dimon would be presented with many opportunities to build companies, gaining expertise not only in making acquisitions, but also in successfully integrating operations and improving efficiency and profitability.

From the early days, Weill and Dimon appeared well-matched: an older, more experienced executive and a very bright and ambitious right-hand man. American Express, however, proved to be a poor fit for Weill. In 1985, Weill resigned from American Express and, despite an attractive offer to remain with the company, Dimon walked out the door with him. For the next year, Weill and Dimon weighed their next move, which turned out to be a Baltimore-based consumer finance firm called Commercial Credit Company. The company was owned at the time by Control Data Corp. Weill presented a proposal whereby Control Data would spin off Commercial Credit, keeping only 20 percent of the company. Weill would become chairman and CEO of Commercial Credit, and his new management team, which included Dimon and several other handpicked executives, would own 10 percent of the firm through stock purchases and option grants. (The remainder of the company was held by shareholders.)

When Commercial Credit needed a chief financial officer, Dimon, then age thirty, stepped into the role for which he was particularly well-suited, given his strong attention to detail and continual focus on identifying and mitigating risks. Titles aside,

Commercial Credit was a no-frills operation where everyone worked hard for a chance to remake a company from the bottom up. Robert "Bob" Lipp, who worked with Dimon in those early days, recalled the fun and hard work of being part of a close-knit team that had taken cuts in salary in order to have a stake in the firm—one they would create and manage their own way. "We were refugees—refugees from bureaucracy," Lipp said in *The House of Dimon*. Lipp described Dimon, who impressed him early on with his hard work and intensity. "He's as smart as can be. He's a quick learner. He did a great amount of study and analysis on his own," Lipp recalled.[3]

Looking back, Dimon described his days at Commercial Credit, "a small third-rate company based in Baltimore," in fond terms. "It is more fun to take something from tenth place to first place, than it is to be born on first place," he said. Commercial Credit would not stay small for long. In 1988, Commercial Credit bought the much larger company Primerica, which had a variety of businesses, including brokerage firm Smith Barney, as well as insurance and mutual fund operations, among other holdings. After the deal, Commercial Credit took on a new name—Primerica—and its management team moved back to New York.

In 1991, Weill promoted Dimon, then thirty-five years old, to be president of Primerica, which made him one of the youngest presidents of a major financial services firm. In an article about the promotion, the *New York Times* called Dimon "one of the most powerful members of his generation on Wall Street,"[4] an observation that seemed to presage future accomplishments. Over the next few years, Primerica grew through a series of acquisitions, including the purchase of Weill's former company, Shearson, from American Express in 1993. Primerica also bought Travelers, a giant in insurance, which resulted in another corporate name change—this time becoming Travelers in 1995.

As the firm grew, so did Dimon's career, in scope and responsibility. In January 1996, while holding the official title of president of Travelers, he also became the head of Smith Barney—a move that signaled he was "coming into his own as a major Wall Street mover and shaker," *BusinessWeek* said at the time. "Dimon has a lot going for him. One asset is his youth. In the stodgy financial-services business, he's on the same wavelength as younger consumers. A technology advocate, he got the firm on the Internet and made it the only brokerage to tie into the popular personal-finance software Quicken. He also pushed Smith Barney to become the first brokerage to sell no-load mutual funds, breaking industry tradition."[5]

The media hailed the growth of Smith Barney, which in 1992 had only 2,000 brokers and a small investment bank. By 1996, following the acquisition of Shearson three years earlier, the firm had 10,500 brokers—in second place behind Merrill Lynch with its 13,000 brokers. "We're becoming a powerhouse," *BusinessWeek* quoted Dimon as saying.[6]

The same was being said for Dimon, himself—an emerging force on Wall Street who was far from being in his boss's shadow.

A Financial Empire Is Created

The more Weill's financial empire grew, the more Dimon had on his plate, not only managing Smith Barney, but another Wall Street "name" as well—Salomon Brothers, which was acquired in 1997. Salomon's Wall Street traders were considered to be among the best and the brightest, and yet, as Dimon would soon see first-hand, the Salomon trading operation also had an appetite for high-risk transactions.

The acquisition of Salomon Brothers also brought another executive into Weill's executive ranks: Deryck Maughan, who had run Salomon. After the deal, Dimon and Maughan were named co-CEOs of the merged operation known as Salomon Smith Barney. Having two executives run an operation can be difficult at times and can set up a scenario for conflict, crossed lines of communication, and confusion among the staff. Publicly, Dimon and Maughan vowed to make the best of it. Behind the scenes, however, tensions were simmering.

In his role as co-CEO of Salomon Smith Barney, Dimon tried to rein in the enormous risks taken by the Salomon traders, while huge positions racked up millions in losses. By late August 1988, despite Dimon's efforts to reduce the risk exposure of Salomon's arbitrage trading group and its speculation in investments such as Russian bonds, Salomon reported a loss estimated at $360 million after taxes in its arbitrage and Russian-related credit businesses for the two prior months.[7]

For Dimon's career, the timing couldn't have been worse. Weill was embarking on the deal of deals—a $70 billion merger of Travelers with Citicorp to form the world's largest financial service company, known as Citigroup. Although he had been at Weill's side from the beginning, it would soon become apparent that Dimon did not have a seat at the table.

The Citigroup Deal

The buying spree that had turned Commercial Credit into Primerica, and then Primerica into Travelers with its huge Salomon Smith Barney operation, was about to reach a pinnacle. In late 1997, Travelers began exploring the possibility of merging with Citicorp. There were serious roadblocks to the merger, including restrictive federal regulations such as the Glass-Steagall Act of 1933, which separated commercial and investment banking and put limits on the financial products that banks could offer. But as the Travelers-Citicorp deal moved forward, history was in the making: a financial colossus the size and scope of which had never been seen before.

The deal was nothing less than a complete change of landscape as banking, brokerage, and insurance were being brought together under one corporate roof. As the New York Times observed, "The Citigroup deal means there is no turning back to the old world of

distinct financial industries where banks compete with one another, while brokerage firms vie with each other and insurance
companies keep to their turf. . . . "[8]

The creation of Citigroup was to be a merger of equals in every
sense of the word, with everything split 50–50. At the top were two
chairmen and co-CEOs: Sandy Weill from Travelers and John
Reed from Citibank. Together, they would share management of
Citigroup. Even the board of directors was being split equally
between the two firms. It was a strategic decision that ultimately
sealed the fate of Citigroup with ineffective management and, some
might say, governance structure. Under the guise of equality, Weill
made Dimon part of a tri-party CEO arrangement and removed him
from the board. In hindsight, it appears to be an ominous sign that
Dimon was being squeezed out of the company he helped to build.

In his book *Last Man Standing*, author Duff McDonald wrote
that, although Dimon was still president of the combined company,
he was not the chief operating officer. In other words, his authority
and responsibilities had been limited. "Despite Weill's trying to
sweet-talk him into believing that the title of president meant he
was well positioned, Dimon saw the empty title for what it was . . .
'I should have realized it when he told me about the board. I should
have left the company at that point. You'd think by then I might
have figured it out, but I didn't,'" McDonald quoted Dimon as
saying.[9]

In our interview, Dimon acknowledged the lesson from that
experience: "When you are in a difficult situation it's hard to think
clearly about it and it's easy to second-guess yourself in retrospect:
why didn't you resign or why didn't you work it out with these guys?
You get so wrapped up in the tension of the moment that it's hard to
step back and see what is really happening and know what to do
about it."

The tri-party CEO arrangement effectively neutralized the
impact and undermined the authority of the individuals involved.
Dimon and Maughan were expected to continue as co-CEOs of the

global corporate unit, which included Salomon Smith Barney and corporate banking. Victor Menezes, who had come from Citicorp, was head of commercial banking and was promoted to be a third CEO. Having three CEOs overseeing the businesses was problematic: "It is too complex. It doesn't work," Dimon said. Having been a co-CEO with Maughan at Salomon Smith Barney was challenging enough; with three "it was exponentially more difficult."

For Dimon, things would only get worse until they reached the breaking point.

The Firing of Jamie Dimon

Over the years, there has been much speculation as to what really led to the firing of Jamie Dimon as president of Citigroup in 1998. Clearly, Dimon's relationship with Weill had deteriorated over the previous two years, creating a rift between them. Some observers point to clashes between Dimon and Maughan as a contributing factor, or perhaps that conflict was an excuse that Weill would use to get rid of Dimon. Another factor could be that Weill disliked the fact that Dimon, who was twenty-three years his junior, was increasingly drawing the spotlight. Whatever the underlying reasons, tensions came to a head in an incident at a corporate retreat in late October 1998 at Greenbrier, an exclusive resort in West Virginia.

As the *New York Times* noted, "Beneath the surface of this ostensibly amiable event, serious trouble was brewing. The day before, Citigroup had posted a huge and disappointing plunge in third-quarter profits, and those ensconced at Greenbrier were soon complaining loudly about the trouble the company was having knitting together such disparate businesses as lending to big companies and bond and stock underwriting."[10] During a social gathering at the retreat, Dimon and Maughan had a confrontation after Maughan apparently snubbed a colleague's wife, and Dimon demanded an apology.

Immediately following the confrontation at the Greenbrier, things seemed to settle down. Dimon had no reason to suspect that, a week or so later, a bombshell would drop.

On Sunday, November 1, 1998, Jamie Dimon and his wife, Judy, hosted a brunch in their home in Manhattan for about 100 Smith Barney recruits. Later that day, a management meeting of the top twenty or so people at Citigroup was scheduled at a conference center in Armonk, New York, about an hour outside the city. In the middle of the brunch at Dimon's home, Sandy Weill called and asked if Dimon would come up to Armonk in the early afternoon, before the management meeting. Dimon agreed. "I took my leave of the group we were hosting in our home and went up to Armonk. I was not suspecting anything," Dimon said.

When he walked into a small conference room in Armonk, Dimon sat down at one side of the table; Weill and Reed were at the other. Weill did most of the talking, as he told Dimon that they wanted to discuss management, adding that he and Reed "have been thinking long and hard about the issue," Dimon recounted. "I had no idea what he was going to say."

At first, Weill outlined a few changes, including the appointment of Michael Carpenter as chairman of Salomon Smith Barney, which had been Dimon's responsibility. "At the time I was thinking, 'I don't know what they're going to do here,'" Dimon said. Weill explained some other corporate reshuffling, including the reassignment of Maughan, who was becoming vice chairman. "Then he said, 'We would like you to resign.' That was the whole conversation," Dimon recalled.

Dimon described experiencing a "funny kind of shock" over what had just happened. However, he also felt a sense of "resolution at the end of a long battle," following a few years of escalating tensions between him and Weill.

Since the management team was about to arrive for the meeting, Dimon stayed to say good-bye to his colleagues. One of the first people he encountered was Bob Lipp, who gave him a hug with tears in his eyes. As the team gathered, Reed explained the decision to ask for Dimon's resignation. Dimon said a few words to his colleagues along the lines of, "John and Sandy have to make decisions like this. This is an outstanding company with outstanding people. If there is anything I can do to help with anything, just ask. . . . "

His first phone call after leaving the conference center was to his wife. Because his habit was often to make jokes he prefaced what he had to say by telling Judy that he was serious: "I was just fired," Dimon told her.

Judy Dimon said she was shocked by the "precise timing of it," although she had had a "sense of foreboding after the Greenbrier situation." "I had this nauseous feeling, although I was not totally conscious of why I had it," she said. Judy was also angered about the way Dimon had been treated. "I didn't feel devastated or anchorless, and I wasn't wringing my hands, I was just angry."

After the initial shock of Dimon losing his job, the impact on him and his family was minimized because, as Judy Dimon explained, "Jamie was totally fine. I never perceived my husband being unwhole at any point—meaning nothing essential about him had been taken away when he was fired."

Judy Dimon's perspective adds an interesting dimension to this story. As many of the executives profiled in this book experienced, when a person is fired or asked to step down or resign, a spouse or other close family member is part of a support system. In Dimon's case, being strongly supported by his family—and, in turn, being supportive of them—helped him weather the transition after Citigroup with a minimum of upset. From the moment he left Citigroup and through the job search process, Judy was Dimon's partner and confidante, a strong bond that was vital since the next job he would chose would impact not just Dimon but the entire family.

When he arrived home in New York, Dimon's first concern was his young daughters, knowing that they would soon hear the news of his firing, perhaps from classmates at school. "I sat the girls down and said, 'I want you to know that I resigned from Citigroup. That really means I was fired. I'm not going to be working there anymore."

Dimon related with good humor the reactions of his young daughters: The youngest, Kara, who was then ten, asked her father if that meant the family would have to live on the street. "No, sweetheart," Dimon assured her. Middle daughter, Laura, who was twelve, asked if they could still go to college. "Absolutely," Dimon replied. Then Julia, the oldest who was fourteen, spoke up: "Since you won't be needing it, can I have your cell phone?" On a more serious note, by telling his young daughters what had happened, Dimon was able to assure them that nothing in their lives had changed just because he was no longer working for Citigroup. This message reflected exactly what Dimon believed about himself.

After the news was announced on Sunday, Dimon, along with Weill and Reed, handled press interviews, presenting a unified front and a peaceful transition. "Both [Weill and Reed] spoke fondly of Mr. Dimon and optimistically of Citigroup's prospects," the New York Times reported. "Mr. Dimon was equally cheery on Sunday, though few on Wall Street accept this friendly chatter as a true indicator of the state of affairs at Citigroup." A Wall Street analyst, commenting on Dimon's departure, called it "a loss of quality management," adding, "Jamie played a significant role in executing the overall strategy. I think you'll see more departures and further turmoil."[11]

On Monday, November 2, Dimon went to the office to pack up his belongings, and fielded "tons of calls and e-mails." As part of his farewell to colleagues and direct reports, Dimon went to the Smith Barney trading floor for the last time. The entire floor gave him a standing ovation. Later that day, a party was held for him, attended by a hundred or more people. "That part was *almost* fun," he recalled.

The next day, Dimon had his first taste of life after Citigroup. The changes were small at first: Instead of reading the newspaper for an hour, he read for two hours. When he went to Central Park for a run, he increased his distance.

"It's not that it didn't hurt, but I knew I was going to be OK. I wasn't going to sit there and cry over it," Dimon reflected.

His comments expanded into a much bigger and broader lesson, not only applicable to dealing with being fired from Citigroup, but also revealing of how he remains grounded even today as a high-profile Wall Street leader. "If you are all wrapped up in a company, if that is the only thing that means something to you, it's a flaw. What about your family and your children, your health, and your country?"

Judy Dimon stressed that Dimon did not need another job to restore or prove himself in any way. What she wanted, however, was a sense of "justice." She explained: "I didn't know what that meant; I didn't have a fixed idea or definition. I wanted to have a feeling inside that justice had prevailed."

In time, Dimon would have his justice, but not without some upheaval and challenges.

Trying on Opportunities

Dimon's departure from Citigroup was not as easy as walking out the door. His severance package and non-compete agreement took about six months to negotiate. The agreement, as Dimon described it, was for a three-year non-compete, involving a "very hard non-compete for a year, a very tough non-solicit prohibiting me from hiring people away from Citigroup for the second year, and a normal non-solicit for the third year." Dimon's attitude toward the agreement was "I wasn't going to raid my former company, and a year wasn't that long a time or that big a deal."

For the first six months, during which the agreement was negotiated, Dimon made a decision not to pursue another job opportunity. Instead, he focused on those things he enjoyed doing, and now could relish since he had more time. His activities were varied, from buying twenty or thirty books—mostly biographies and history—to boxing. During the summer of 1999, Dimon took his family on a five-week trip to Europe, visiting London, Paris, Venice, Florence, and Rome—all with "no real big agenda, just exploring on our own." Come September, when his children were back in school, Dimon told himself, he would start thinking more seriously about his next job.

At the end of 1999, Dimon invited Weill to lunch, the first attempt at peacemaking between the two. "We talked about the past for about two minutes. Then I said, 'Look, whether I was to blame or you were to blame, or it was sixty–forty or forty–sixty, it doesn't matter," Dimon recalled telling Weill. "I don't believe that what you did was the right thing for the company, but here are the mistakes that I made. And that was the end of it."

Dimon's ability to move beyond being fired stemmed from the fact that he did not feel victimized. As Judy commented, "Things were different, so now what were we going to do about it?" Judy also offered advice to others who are supporting someone going through a career upheaval. "You must find a passion of your own that will empower you to be strong and helpful to your spouse," she added. For Judy Dimon, educational reform and community development have always been and remain strong interests.

As Dimon looked ahead, several possibilities were presented to him: European investment banks, divisions of large financial services firms, an insurance company. "I talked to a lot of people. There were even some jobs that were offered to me that could have hurt my feelings, but I talked to them anyway," Dimon said. His discernment process to evaluate professional opportunities was deliberate, and he avoided any temptation to fill up his calendar by joining boards or becoming an advisor. This experience is the essence of the advice he gives to others who are suddenly in a career transition: "Take a deep breath and take your time. Don't be a cork in the ocean—decide where you are going. Otherwise, before you know it, you have joined a bunch of boards because you are trying to fill up your time. You didn't decide. It was decided for you."

One intriguing possibility was to become the second in command at Amazon. Dimon flew out to Seattle to meet CEO Jeff Bezos, and the two men quickly hit it off, but more on a personal level than as partners in a management team. Dimon later called Bezos and declined any further discussions because he believed that the job at Amazon would be just "too far afield" from his expertise in financial services.

Another opportunity Dimon considered very seriously was joining The Home Depot to become the "Number Two" to the CEO, Arthur Blank. Dimon recalled conversations with Blank and Bernard Marcus, who along with Kenneth Langone had founded the firm. "I loved those guys—their ethics and values, and it's a great company," Dimon remarked.

If Dimon were to take a job with Home Depot, it would impact the family; therefore, Judy was an integral part of the decision-making process. The Dimons considered this opportunity seriously enough to look at houses in the Atlanta area where The Home Depot is based, and to consider what living in the South would be like for the family. It was all part of the process that Dimon described as "trying them on": imagining what it would be like to live the life that came with a particular job. "What time would I wake up in the morning? How much would I be traveling? How would the job demands impact my kids?"

Although Home Depot would have offered "a great life," in the end Dimon decided against it because he did not know the business well enough. "It's like when you take a golfer and say, 'Now you've got to learn baseball,'" he said. Dimon's game had always been financial services, and that is where he would stay.

Joining Bank One

In early 2000, with the rigorous non-compete provisions no longer in force, Dimon was approached by an executive recruiter representing the search committee of the board of Bank One, a regional bank based in Chicago that was in the midst of recruiting a new CEO. Bank One had been formed by the merger of First Chicago NBD of Chicago and Banc One of Columbus, Ohio. The two banks, however, had never been fully integrated—not in operations (for example, information technology systems from both companies were largely incompatible) and certainly not from the perspective of corporate culture. Bank One's troubles began to escalate in the second half of 1999 after the company announced that its earnings would be less than expected due to a lackluster performance in its credit card and consumer loan portfolio. The CEO stepped down in 1999, and an interim executive was put in place.

As the board began its search for a new CEO, Jamie Dimon emerged as a strong contender because of his deep knowledge of the financial services industry and his experience with so many acquisitions and integrations over years, especially during his time at Primerica/Travelers. What made him distinct in the eyes of the search committee were his ability to drive execution throughout an organization and his moral courage that guides him to do the right thing. As James Crown, who had been on the Bank One board and served on the search committee, stated in *The House of Dimon*, "Jamie came out of this [candidate interview] process as just a white-hot, superior level of intelligence, very knowledgeable about financial services, the securities industry, and banking, and as a tireless worker."

The fact that the job was in Chicago, however, was a drawback for the Dimons. "It was hard. If I had a choice, I really wouldn't have moved," Dimon admitted. Moving from New York to Chicago meant leaving extended family and close friends and upsetting normal life routines.

Judy Dimon echoed his thoughts, adding, "I had no idea what I was getting into with the relocation. I had relocated as a single person and even as a married person, but this time around we were moving our daughters at a formative time in their lives. They would be entering sixth, eighth, and tenth grades and would be making a transition from an all girls' school in New York to a co-educational school in Chicago. For me, the prospect of leaving family and friends and a community I loved was daunting."

Although the move created an upheaval in their lives, Dimon and his wife recognized that if he wanted to stay in financial services it was necessary to look beyond New York City. "How many big financial companies are out there? Twenty or thirty? How many would be changing CEOs in the next two or three years, maybe four or five? How many would hire from the outside, one or two?" Dimon stated.

Although the widely held view was that Dimon had been fired from Citigroup for political reasons, not because of a performance issue, it was a slight taint to his reputation, which might have been enough to turn away a large, healthy institution in search of a CEO. Given all these factors, the Bank One job was the best opportunity out there.

Paul W. Marshall, Professor of Management Practice at Harvard Business School, observed that, given Dimon's background, his high energy level, and his relative young age of forty-four at the time, he was well suited to tackle the Bank One turnaround. "There is something in Jamie Dimon's makeup, whether it's genetic or environmental, that makes him very competitive with a high desire to win."

There are other facets of Dimon's personality that weighed in his favor, including a strong work ethic and a high degree of candor—traits that he still exhibits today. "The other characteristic that I see in leaders who take on a turnaround is they are candid. They look at the work that needs to be done and tell people what they see. That helps them gain trust, particularly when it was a bad situation," Marshall added.

When Dimon took over as chairman and CEO of Bank One in March 2000, he never pulled any punches over the challenges he faced from the first day. As he observed in his 2004 speech at Northwestern, "Aggressive accounting, a disjointed board, horrible credit problems that could have sunk the company, not enough capital, awful customer service, disjointed systems. . . . "[13] Turning around the bank would be an enormous undertaking.

From the start, Dimon continued his mantra to "do the right thing," a phrase he still uses frequently, which carries implications from ethical standards to customer service. At Bank One, doing the "right thing" meant improving efficiencies, cutting unnecessary expenses, extending branch hours, being more responsive to customers, and demanding accountability throughout the organization. Dimon showed himself to be a tough, demanding boss at Bank One— constantly asking questions, probing deeply, uncovering problems, and demanding solutions—but also a highly committed CEO.

Back to New York

The turnaround of Bank One took three years, but the results were worth the wait. In 2000, Dimon's first year as CEO of Bank One, the company posted a $511 million loss. Three years after— following management changes and a reduction of $1.5 billion of unnecessary expenses—the result was a $3.5 billion profit in 2003. At last, Bank One was healthy enough to consider expanding further by making an acquisition. Instead, in 2004 it was acquired: a $58 billion deal with JPMorgan Chase. Jamie Dimon was headed back to New York, a move that *Time* magazine called "a triumphant return."[14]

Fortune chimed in with its praise, noting "the deal replicates what Dimon and his mentor Sandy Weill succeeded in doing five years ago, when Travelers Group, the brokerage, investment-banking, and insurance conglomerate they had built over the previous decade, bought retail titan Citicorp to form Citigroup."[15]

The acquisition of Bank One by JPMorgan was viewed as a crowning achievement at the time for Dimon, and certainly put him back in the spotlight in the heart of the financial services industry. However, the Dimons now faced the decision of how to handle this new job in the context of family life and the fact that the youngest daughters were still in high school. Over the years, the family had grown attached to their friends and life in Chicago. This time around, their daughters' best interests were the family's priority: Judy and the girls would stay in Chicago while Dimon commuted to New York every week, returning on the weekends, until the youngest daughter graduated from high school in 2007. "He did that every week and he didn't skip a beat—ever," Judy explained. "I think he really needed to touch home base to refuel. The family for him is his avocation, his interest, and his passion."

As part of the merger agreement, Dimon would become the number two executive at JPMorgan Chase, working with William Harrison, who was the chairman and CEO. If everything went well, Dimon would take over as CEO and chairman when Harrison retired in mid-2006. The two men worked exceptionally well together, and Harrison was highly supportive of Dimon and respected his leadership abilities. In fact, Harrison commented that he considered Dimon "the best successor I could have found in the business world."[16] For his part, Dimon credits Harrison for having an influence on his leadership. "Bill Harrison is such a gentleman. He made it so easy to do the merger," he added.

In his role as president at JPMorgan, Dimon undertook a campaign to reduce unnecessary costs and improve competitiveness, much as he did at Bank One. As Dimon took on more of the day-to-day management, the transition from Harrison to Dimon was moved up by mutual agreement to the end of 2005, when he became chairman and CEO of JPMorgan Chase.

Since taking the reins at JPMorgan Chase, it has been quite a ride for Dimon, including weathering a brutal financial crisis that caused the failure of two venerable investment banks—Bear Stearns, which was acquired by JPMorgan Chase in March 2008 in a deal that was facilitated by the Treasury Department and the Federal Reserve, and Lehman Brothers, which went bankrupt in September 2008. Throughout the crisis, eyes have been largely on Dimon.

Dimon has been hailed in the media and even among some lawmakers (despite a political climate that has leveled criticism at Wall Street bankers). The *Financial Times* included Dimon on its list of "50 People Who Will Frame the Way Forward" after the financial crisis, ranking him among a who's who of government, economic, and business leaders worldwide.[17]

Reflecting on his career, Dimon shrugged off the accolades as he stated his pride for "this place—JPMorgan—not me." He said, "I think we have built a company that the country can be proud of, a company that represents opportunity for people and that treats people with respect."

Although Dimon is often lauded for his leadership, and has received numerous awards and honors as a CEO, he readily credits the influence of others. "I learned a lot from Sandy Weill. He had guts and an unbelievable work ethic. I also learned the things not to do from Sandy. Both of those were good lessons," Dimon observed.

Another strong influence has been Bob Lipp, a colleague from the Commercial Credit days, who also served as a special advisor and member of the board of JPMorgan Chase. "Bob has a wonderful way about him—his discipline about reviewing businesses and his love of getting out in the field, how he treats everyone."

Other leaders whom Dimon admires include Warren Buffett, a "brilliant thinker," as well as Charlie Munger, who with Buffett runs Berkshire Hathaway. He called the late Andrall "Andy" Pearson, a former president of PepsiCo who became the founding chairman of Yum! Brands, "one of the most talented executives I ever saw." Dimon said he "learned a lot" from former General Electric CEO Jack Welch, particularly by reading about his leadership. An avid student of history, Dimon also has been influenced by leaders such as Abraham Lincoln and Nelson Mandela. "When you read about them in detail, you see what they went through and how they dealt with situations," Dimon added.

As for his own views on leadership, Dimon emphasizes privilege and responsibility, which are inseparable. As he summarized in a speech to Harvard Business School graduates in June 2009, "It is an honor, a privilege and a very deep responsibility to be a leader, whether of a small group or a larger company. You have to remind yourself, if you make a mistake, you could hurt a lot of people: customers, communities, shareholders, employees, parents. I worry about this every single day."[18]

Dimon, who turned fifty-four in March 2010, offered no hints about what his future might bring, other than to restate the priorities that have governed all his decisions and his commitment to keep doing what he's been doing. "I love my family. I love my country. I love this company. As long as I am at JPMorgan, I am going to work as hard as I can to make this a great company."

Jamie Dimon is the ultimate comeback story, but not solely because of the success he now enjoys as the chairman and CEO of a leading financial services institution. He takes his responsibilities seriously because he understands their impact on the company, the community, and the country. Moreover, he never loses sight of the fact that who he is as a person and his relationship with his family define him—not his job title. Although he is viewed as being on top in the financial world, Dimon's feet are firmly on the ground.

I had never worked for money, but for the challenge and the passion and the learning curve. . . . When the curve went flat, I went to find something else. . . . I asked myself, why do I do what I do? What do I really want to do and, the most compelling question of all, what am I going to become passionate about?

—DALE DAWSON,
FORMER CEO OF TRUCKPRO, L.P. AND
FORMER HEAD OF INVESTMENT BANKING FOR
STEPHENS INC.

Chapter Ten

DALE DAWSON
PURSUING A LIFE OF PASSION

From the day Dale Dawson graduated from the University of Texas with a master's degree in taxation and finance in 1975, he rocketed along the fast track. At each juncture of his career, Dawson was spurred on by the need to be continuously engaged and intellectually challenged. With his energy and intelligence, Dawson segued from one opportunity to the next, never afraid to try something new. The steeper the learning curve, the happier he was. Being bored was a consequence far worse than failure.

Following graduation, Dawson joined the Big Eight accounting firm, Peat, Marwick, Mitchell & Co., which later became KPMG, and rose through the ranks of the firm's insurance practice, which was exploding at the time with a spate of mergers and acquisitions (M&A) in the insurance industry. When he looked around for the next challenge in the mid-1980s, he decided to join Stephens Inc., a highly successful and well-respected private investment firm in Little Rock, Arkansas, where he helped to grow its investment banking and M&A advisory businesses.

That's how in 1991, while at Stephens Inc., Dawson found an attractive investment opportunity and his next big move: a heavy-duty truck parts distributor called TruckPro. As a significant share-holder, Dawson decided to take on the role of a hands-on CEO, and over the next two years he turned the operation around and improved its profitability. Then, in 1998, at the age of forty-six,

Dawson sold the company, which by then had about $150 million in annual sales, and stepped off the career track.

Suddenly Dawson found himself in an uncomfortable transition like none he had ever experienced. The next new challenge was not at hand. It was as though his world, previously so full of activity, ideas, and interactions, had gone silent. Dawson had no idea what he wanted to do next. He and his wife, Judi, had made enough money over the years to support their lifestyle. Yet he knew that material things would not satisfy the deeper hunger that gnawed at him. He was poor in what mattered the most: passion and purpose. "When you are passionate, your energy is so high. You're thinking ten steps ahead, trying to figure things out," Dawson said.

At mid-life, however, Dawson had lost that passion. Without it, he was uncertain of how to move himself forward. He was stuck, and he desperately needed to reignite what had always motivated him. But rediscovering passion wasn't as easy as finding another job or a company to run. It was a gift, which he had always taken for granted.

Unlike other executives interviewed for this book who endured some type of career upset caused by external factors—many of which were beyond their control—Dawson was the cause of his own turmoil. He could have stayed with the status quo with a career in investment banking or bought another company. Instead, he pulled the proverbial rug out from under himself because he knew that what had come before was no longer satisfying. His only choice was to embark on a journey away from the familiar and well off the path he had followed so successfully since college. He made a leap of faith into the unknown in order for his purpose to be revealed. What he found changed his life—and quite possibly the world.

Getting Up Before Everyone Else

To Dale Dawson, his father was the hardest working man he ever met. An independent milk distributor for Borden in Snyder, Texas, a town of 12,000 between Lubbock and Abilene, his father got up at three o'clock in the morning, worked until noon, napped for thirty minutes, and then went back to work and collected milk bills in the evening. His mother, whom his father had put through Texas Tech University where she majored in accounting, took care of the bills and the bookkeeping. "I remember thinking, 'My Dad is the hardest working man in this town,' and that was pretty cool. Nobody works six days a week and starts working at three o'clock in the morning," Dawson recalled.

The oldest of three brothers, Dawson fondly remembers getting up before dawn to help his father. By five in the morning, the two of them would set out in the truck. The back doors of the houses were usually open, and it was not uncommon for the Dawsons to let themselves in and put the milk in the refrigerator. For the younger Dawson, it was first-hand indoctrination in his father's work ethics and values: what mattered most were commitment to family and hard work.

By the time he was in high school, Dawson moved with his family to Houston after his father went to work for Borden to establish a retail milk distribution business in that city. Later, Dawson entered the University of Texas, where he started out as a psychology major— a self-described "Jesus freak hippie," living in a communal house, with long hair down his back, and spending his free time remodeling a coffeehouse. Then one day, while sitting on the porch, he met a group of young men from a fraternity who were walking by, accompanied by very attractive young women. Dawson invited them to sit on the porch to have a beer. As they relaxed, the young men from the fraternity began complaining about their studies in accounting.

"They were moaning about how hard it was and that they didn't know if they could get it," Dawson recalled. Then he got an idea: "I had been keeping books since I was about ten. I thought to myself, why aren't I whipping these guys?"

Dawson changed his major, cut his hair, and in 1974 graduated near the top of his class in accounting. A year later, he received his master's degree and went to work at KPMG in Dallas, which was one of the firm's leading offices in the United States, with large practices in oil and gas, banking, and real estate. When a young partner in the insurance practice convinced him to join that group, Dawson decided to specialize in corporate insurance tax. It was highly complicated but for Dawson strongly appealing because of the intellectual challenge. His goal was nothing less than to become an expert in the field. "I remember sitting by the pool, studying corporate tax," he joked.

A wave of M&A activity in the insurance industry brought the practice into prominence at KPMG. Soon Dawson was traveling the country, consulting with clients, and working on deals. After only six years with the firm, he made partner at the age of thirty. Two years later, he was national director of the insurance practice. Then Dawson ran out of challenges. "I got bored," he remembered. "I had been promoted every year of my life from kindergarten until I was thirty-two. There was nothing else to get promoted to."

M&A tax consulting, however, had put Dawson in touch with investment bankers from many of the leading firms. It was his "back door introduction" to a field in which he could apply his knowledge and expertise. An invitation came from Jack Stephens, a partner with his brother Witt in the investment firm Stephens Inc. Over the years, Stephens Inc., which had started in municipal bonds, had expanded into private equity. In 1970, the firm took Wal-Mart public. By the mid-1980s, it had become more active in investment banking, which was headed by Jack Stephens's son, Warren Stephens. Stephens Inc. had always prided itself on its independence and on building long-term relationships with clients in the United States and abroad who appreciated the firm's values and emphasis on long-term results. Jack approached Dawson with a proposition: to build an M&A advisory business. "Jack had always worked with friends giving them advice on M&A, but he found it awkward to hand them a bill," Dawson recalled. "He said to me,

'You don't seem to have any trouble giving out bills. Come here and help Warren build the business.'"

Joining Stephens Inc. in 1985 meant moving to Little Rock, Arkansas. His wife, Judi, whom he had met at KPMG where she was an auditor, had left the firm and had her own lighting business, partnering with her former boss to import ceiling fans and track lighting, which she sold in stores in Texas and Denver. Soon after Dawson and his wife relocated, competition from Wal-Mart and Home Depot ruined the viability of Judi's lighting business, which was saddled with $1 million in debt and inventory that needed to be discounted and sold.

"We closed the worst-performing store, put the inventory in a truck and brought it to the next store to sell it. I was doing deals alongside top Wall Street firms and building the M&A practice at Stephens Inc. during the week, and on Friday nights I was loading trucks and selling off inventory," Dawson recalled. "The debt and the inventory evened out in about nine months. But we were busted. At least I had a future at Stephens."

Indeed, Dawson had a very bright future with Stephens as the M&A practice grew. For example, when Tenneco Inc., a large diversified industrial company, divested five insurance companies to I.C.H. Corporation, an insurance holding company, for about $1.5 billion in 1986, Stephens Inc. made a tidy $6 million advisory fee. "I had been there about 18 months by then. Jack said, 'I am really liking this business,'" Dawson recalled. "We really worked hard to become a boutique in M&A, working with clients such as Tyson Foods and Alltel Corporation [an Arkansas-based telecommunication company that was later acquired by Verizon]."

Dawson's success at Stephens Inc. continued. When Warren Stephens became president of the firm, Dawson was promoted to become head of the investment banking practice. Judi Dawson, meanwhile, also went to work for Stephens Inc., becoming a stockbroker. Within a few years, she was the number one salesperson, Dawson noted proudly. After the stock-market crash of

1987, the Stephens Inc. broker in London quit. Judi volunteered to take that book of business over, working with clients such as Scottish pension funds that had made good returns investing through Stephens Inc. in Arkansas-based companies.

In short, life was good. In 1991, Dawson became a father for a second time with the birth of his son, Jack. His daughter, Katherine, was two. Then six months later, Dawson's world was rocked by the death of his father at the age of sixty-three. "For a year after my Dad died, I cried every time I was alone. I realized that his attitude and view of life, his values and how he lived, were imprinted on my mind at a level and a depth that I wasn't even aware of—and this was a man I hadn't lived with since I left for college. Yet, he was still having an impact on me," Dawson said. "What I learned then was that the people on whom I would have the most impact in my life were my children."

In hindsight, this was the beginning of an awakening and a shift in priorities for Dawson, although he could not fully see or appreciate it at the time. Instead, what he was most aware of was the fact that he was getting bored at Stephens. The investment banking business, while financially rewarding, no longer held an intellectual challenge. Dawson's response was to find a new opportunity for himself: a heavy-duty truck parts distributor, which had been founded as Haygood Truck & Trailer Parts in 1958 and later became TruckPro. Dale and Judi Dawson became significant shareholders, along with the Stephens family, its executives, and some private equity investors.

Three months later, the chief financial officer of TruckPro told Dawson that the company was going to fail. It was the spark he needed to get into action. "I was not going to let it go bankrupt," Dawson explained. "This was my chance to fix something as an operator."

Dawson left Stephens's investment banking practice and became the full-time CEO of TruckPro, which at the time had about $60 million in sales. After replacing the management team, he rolled up his sleeves to undertake a turnaround of a business in an industry of which he had no knowledge. As he dove into the operations, Dawson discovered widespread problems. "Not one aspect of that company was running well—accounting, information technology, human resources, compensation . . . ," he said. "Over the next four to five years, I went into every single aspect of running that company. I completely redesigned the inventory management system and the pricing system."

Dawson trained young managers to read financial statements, making them accountable for the results produced by their stores. Within six months, a new discipline was created among the managers who not only could understand the financial statements, but also manage according to them. For Dawson, his role as a teacher and mentor not only improved the business, it also demonstrated his capacity to teach and inspire others—skills that would become important later on. For the moment, however, all Dawson could focus on was getting TruckPro back on track.

When the turnaround was complete, TruckPro had grown from about twenty stores located in the South to fifty stores in the Midwest from Cleveland to just south of Chicago, and in the South from Carolina to Florida and over to Texas. Margins had improved and return on investment was good. But the company's top line could not surpass $150 million. "I couldn't make the business grow any more," Dawson explained.

The only way to get to the next level would be to combine with a larger firm. Dawson had his sights on AutoZone, a retail auto parts business that had seen explosive growth, with 1,936 stores selling auto parts, chemicals, and accessories in thirty-eight states. In March 1998, AutoZone agreed to acquire TruckPro. In a statement, John C. Adams, Jr., chairman and CEO of AutoZone, stressed the opportunity that TruckPro presented. "Getting into the heavy-duty parts business is a natural extension of our strengths," Adams said. "When you combine TruckPro's depth of knowledge in heavy-duty parts with our knowledge of a similar business and our systems expertise, you've got a winning combination."[1]

With TruckPro sold, Dawson looked around to see what was next. Judi, meanwhile, had taken a sabbatical from Stephens Inc. to spend more time with their children, then aged six and eight. "We said, 'Let's just pause and play with our children and figure out what life is all about," Dawson recalled.

What was supposed to be a welcome break turned into an uncomfortable transition during which Dawson would have to delve deep to discover what he would do next. The answer would take him to places he never dreamed.

In Pursuit of Passion

During this transition in his career, Dawson continually confronted himself with the question of what he should pursue as his next opportunity. "I had always wanted to be a Texas wheeler-dealer, buying and selling businesses, and putting deals together," he reflected. When he stepped back and thought about what he wanted to do, however, that dream was less appealing. He already had enough money to sustain his current lifestyle without going back to work. Although he had financial freedom and was without pressure to jump to the next thing, Dawson felt disoriented and vulnerable.

"I had never worked for money, but for the challenge and the passion and the learning curve as a top tax guy, a partner in the investment banking business putting deals together, turning around companies, building an inventory and a pricing system. . . . There was always an enormous learning curve," Dawson added. "When the curve had gone flat at KPMG and then at Stephens, I went to find something else to do."

This time, however, it was different; nothing captured Dawson's interest the way earlier opportunities had. "During this period of reorienting, I asked myself, why do I do what I do? What do I really want to do and, the most compelling question of all, what am I going to become passionate about?"

At first, Dawson decided to go back to work for Stephens Inc. to run the investment banking practice. "During my absence, the investment banking team had exploded. When I left there were about twenty bankers; when I came back there were sixty bankers," he said. But even the growth of the firm failed to adequately engage him. What was missing was the challenge of learning something new. As Dawson put it, "I could do this without getting up early in the morning. I didn't have to work on weekends. It was not stretching me."

What made it hard to walk away, however, was the fact that Stephens was "a wonderful place to work" and Dawson personally liked Warren Stephens, who was now president of the firm. "It was a very confusing time for me. It should have been the time to cash in and make a lot of money," Dawson added. Instead, he was unhappy. No matter how hard he tried, he could no longer deny that something was missing.

He came to realize that his passion, which he always thought was self-generated, was actually something that came to him as if from an external source. This epiphany was part of a deeper spiritual awakening. Although he would not have described himself at the time as particularly religious, Dawson had the feeling that there was something beyond him that was in control of his life and his passion.

"I remember telling someone that it was like I was in a hot air balloon. I'm in the basket. The flame keeps coming on and off, raising and lowering the balloon, but I'm not the one doing that," Dawson said. "As I approached the age of fifty, I started to see that passion was divinely gifted. Looking back, I could see that there had been no time in my life when I could keep the passion when it went away. I had this sense of vulnerability, because I knew what fuels the joy in my life was something that I was not in control of."

Several circumstances came together unexpectedly that would shape the course of Dawson's life. At the time, however, he was not aware of their importance. It began with a woman name Martha Vetter, who taught a children's Bible study for Dawson's daughter and her twelve-year-old friends. Martha told them she was going to Rwanda to help Bishop John Rucyahana with the boarding school he had built for orphans to help restore his country after the devastating genocide of 1994. Martha had a background in nursing and elementary education, as well as ministry. Bishop John needed her and, at the age of forty-two, she was going to go.

"It was like somebody threw a rock through our window," Dawson remembered. "This was a normal person, and she had this sense of calling; that God wanted her to pack up and walk away from everybody she knew and move to Africa. She was passionate for it, I could tell. The danger and the problems and the challenges she would face didn't make any difference."

Dawson, however, did not want her to go. Martha was a friend, and he hated the fact that his daughter would no longer have the experience of studying with her. Despite his negative feelings about her decision to leave, when Martha said that Bishop John Rucyahana was coming to Little Rock, Dawson and his wife agreed to host a dinner to help him raise $700,000 to build a high school. The cause was a worthy one: Without a place to pursue their education, the orphans in Bishop John's primary school would have few alternatives other than returning to the streets.

Dawson believed his personal involvement with Bishop John's cause would end with hosting a dinner and inviting friends to meet him. What he didn't count on was the indelible and lasting impression that Bishop John would make on him. "When he came to my house, he started describing his vision to me: to build the best school in the country, a place to groom leaders," Dawson said. "In Rwanda, if you could create fifty college-bound kids, you can create the next generation of leaders."

As Bishop John spoke, Dawson could see that he had passion—the spark of inspiration that had been missing in his own life for the past few years. "I thought, this guy is brilliant. He's as good as any entrepreneur I had ever worked with," he recalled.

Two other realizations struck Dawson. One, as an investment banker, when he finds a gifted entrepreneur, his instinct is to become that person's partner. The other realization was that Bishop John's activities were totally directed toward others, with no desire for personal accomplishment or reward. "The thought hit me, when Bishop John goes to heaven he's going to get a lot of 'attaboys.' There was nothing I was doing in my life that was worth an 'attaboy' compared to him," Dawson admitted.

In October 2002, at the age of fifty, Dale Dawson made a monumental admission: He had been treading water, completely helpless to find his own way forward. The only way to regain passion in his life was, as he saw it, for God to give it to him. Otherwise, he could only hope to linger in an unsatisfying status quo.

Dawson was also influenced at the time by a book called *Halftime: Moving from Success to Significance*, by Bob Buford, founder of the Halftime Institute, which helps people find significance in the second half of their lives. In his opening pages, Buford wrote of experiences that were incredibly familiar to Dawson: "I started to wrestle with what I wanted out of the second half of my life. I was gripped with an unformed but very compelling idea that I should make my life truly productive, not merely profitable."[2]

The dissatisfaction Dawson felt with his life certainly had nothing to do with a lack of success. He had achieved multiple accomplishments, including running a well-regarded investment banking practice and turning around a company that could then be sold to a fast-growing firm. The wall he hit was, in many ways, a result of all those accomplishments and a sense that there is nothing more to do other than repeat the same. As Buford explained in an interview, "Many people just tire of working. Many of them are drawn to something beyond compulsive success to a sense of service to other people. You get bored with mastery. It's a paradox and a surprise. You think 'been there and done that,' and you wonder what is next. Something draws you forward."

Dawson was struck by the fact that he was not the first person to hit midlife with an upset, whether due to the loss of a job, a health issue, or, like him, facing an uncertain fork in the road. High-achievers were always accelerating along the curve of achievement, trying to get to some end point faster. All he was doing, he learned from Buford, was racing ahead to the point where the curve would eventually flatten and go down. After that point, there would be loss: perhaps one's health, one's family, and sense of self-worth. "Before you get to that point," Dawson explained, "you need to reassess: use your skills and your talent to be of service to somebody else."

Although he had no desire to become a missionary or travel to Africa, Dawson decided to pursue the only opportunity before him where he hoped to regain his passion: that was to help Bishop John realize his vision in Rwanda. In order to do that, however, Dawson would have to finally leave behind his familiar world at Stephens Inc.

"Your work and your career are your identity," Dawson explained. "For me, that was being the head of the investment banking team at Stephens in Little Rock, Arkansas. We had this lifestyle. I was partners with people I admired and liked."

As he wrestled with his decision to resign from the firm, Dawson said he received the best advice from Judi, whom he describes as "the most fearless person in the whole world." "She told me, 'You need to do what you love. Nothing else matters.'"

In October 2003, he stepped down as the head of the invest-ment banking practice at Stephens Inc. He leaped into a void of his own creation: making himself available to whatever would happen next.

Purpose for the Second Half of Life

For Dawson, leaving Stephens Inc. a second time was the hardest decision. Previously when he left the firm, it was to run TruckPro as the CEO. Now he had nothing else to do other than some yet-to-be-defined charity work. Instead of going to the office every day, he was at home without a routine, structure, or support system. For a man who got up early every day to devote his time and energy to the challenge at hand, being idle was torture—and yet it was also incredibly freeing.

The well-intentioned but misguided advice he encountered from some people was that if he wanted to do good works, being in a prestigious job at a place like Stephens would give him the platform he needed. Dawson, however, saw it differently: He needed to give up the job and the title and look elsewhere for his purpose and identity. "You ask yourself, can you walk away from this stuff? It's not really important. It isn't who you are," he said.

When Bishop John visited Little Rock for a second fundraiser, Dawson told him he was available to help in any way. Bishop John's response was immediate. "He told me, 'Well, you are a business guy. The thing I am concerned about the most is that no matter how good our schools are, if Rwanda doesn't have a vibrant economy, the best and the brightest from our country will end up working in North America or Europe. You are a businessman. You build and finance businesses. Why don't you spend the rest of your life building businesses in Rwanda?'"

By early 2004, Dawson had taken Bishop John's challenge to heart, lending his support to Rwandan projects. At the same time, he became involved with a group called Opportunity International, which provides microfinance to people in developing countries who want to start and grow their own businesses. In order to contribute, Dawson, who had taken on challenges from corporate tax to investment banking, would become an expert in microfinance. Suddenly his life path up to that point made perfect sense to him. "At that moment I felt that God had leaned down to me and said, 'You realize that I have been preparing you to do this work from the day you were born, from when you watched your mother work the adding machine. Now you will help people who want to be entrepreneurs to make enough money to feed their kids,'" Dawson reflected.

Dawson interpreted his breakthrough through the lens of his faith. But others who seek to change the course of their lives in order to serve others may see their breakthroughs in other contexts. What is universal, however, is how talent, previous experiences, and a network of contacts may uniquely position a person for new undertakings in philanthropy.

With a new devotion to microfinance, Dawson's passion was back. After a first trip to Mexico with Opportunity International, where Dawson advised a woman who had started a business selling candy, he knew he had found his calling for the second half of his life. Dawson became more involved with Opportunity International, going on the road to tell other business leaders in the States about the group's mission. Then, in October 2004, he made his first trip to Africa. He visited Rwanda, where Bishop John had begun to realize his vision with the construction of a high school. He traveled to Uganda where a boarding school had been established for fifty boys in their last two years of high school. Speaking with these youths, Dawson was struck by their commitment and purpose. This visit gave him a crystal-clear picture of what was also possible in Rwanda, where Bishop John planned to graduate a hundred students a year. These young people, committed to their country and to each other, would be the future leaders who could make a difference in Rwanda, across Africa, and in the world.

By this point, Dawson had also met Bob Buford, who had asked him to join the board of Halftime. Buford helped Dawson articulate a mission statement for himself, as he described it, "not to tell you what to do, but what not to do." Drawing on a white board, Dawson came up with a compelling image that led him to his mission statement: a globe with the United States on one side and Africa on the other. "The vision was to build a bridge, from here to there, and transform people's lives on both ends of the bridge," Dawson explained.

Dawson's commitment to building a bridge between the States and Africa has been possible because he has grasped four key elements of the halftime journey, which Bob Buford described as "capacity, core, context and courage."

Capacity relates directly to one's financial resources and control of one's time; the means that a person has amassed during the first half of life, a portion of which can now be put to another use. Core is one's identity, which extends well beyond job title to a person's strengths. Too often, Buford observed, people become so defined by their roles that they are unable to see themselves in any other capacity. Out of touch with who they are and unaware of their strengths, they cannot see the gifts and talents that they can contribute in other ways.

Context is how and where a person is going to carry out his or her passion, to "do whatever noble thing they want to do," Buford explained. "Dale is totally energized by Rwanda," he cited as an example. Courage is a leap of faith, which does not necessarily mean religious faith. Rather, it connotes going into something without being altogether certain of the process or outcome. For some, this is a voluntary transition brought on by a desire to do something new and more socially significant. For others, it may be brought on by an external event that causes them to rethink their lives, whether a heart attack, reaching a certain age, or a career disruption.

"This journey is a kind of obstacle course that has to do with getting control of your capacity, understanding your strengths (core), finding a context, and having the raw guts to go for it," Buford said. That explanation is illustrated by the journey to which Dawson is fully committed: using the capacity from a successful career and his core skills as a dealmaker in the context of Rwanda, with a great deal of courage.

To carry out his vision, Dawson has partnered with Bishop John Rucyahana as the cofounders of "Bridge2Rwanda" (www .bridge2rwanda.org), which seeks to create the next generation of leaders in the country who are focused on service to others. Describing the mission of Bridge2Rwanda, Dawson quotes two of the most influential and inspirational people he has ever met. "Bishop John has a saying: 'We are not educating students to be job seekers, but rather job creators.' President Paul Kagame [of Rwanda] says, 'Our prosperity will be driven by our success in the private sector,'" Dawson explained. "Our job is to identify the best and the brightest young people, get them the education and the work experience, mold them to be the servant leaders the country requires, and reengage them back in the economy. That's the bridge. That's our focus."

In 2005, Dawson went back to Rwanda with Judi and their two children, along with Scott Ford, a friend who was the CEO at Alltel, and his three sons. President Kagame extended a dinner invitation to both families. At the end of the evening, they reciprocated, inviting the president to visit them in Arkansas. A month later, President Kagame contacted them: In September 2005 he was going to be at the United Nations and wanted to spend the weekend in Little Rock.

Inspired by Bishop John and President Kagame, Dawson became even more involved in Rwanda. He arranged for a feasibility study to be conducted for Opportunity International, which up to that point had not been involved in Rwanda. The study clearly showed the potential to help a nascent private sector with loans, savings, and other financial services. In 2007, Opportunity International merged with three other Christian relief organizations—World Relief, World Relief Canada, and HOPE International—to establish the Urwego Opportunity Bank of Rwanda, headquartered in the capital city of Kigali.

In our interview, Dawson took none of the credit for the bank or for raising more than $5 million to fund it, although it was clear he had a hand in the undertaking. Instead, he pointed out that his friends, Dabbs Calvin and Todd Brogdon, had moved their families from Little Rock to Rwanda to start Urwego Opportunity Bank. The four groups that partnered on the bank, however, cited Dawson as the genesis of the idea. In a press release the organizations noted, "Ironically, this unique partnership did not begin in any of the partnering organizations, but with the dream of a former investment banker from Little Rock, Ark., Dale Dawson, a dedicated volunteer . . . " Dawson's statement in the press release about the Urwego Opportunity Bank drew attention to the needs in Rwanda, his number one priority. "We believe we can be a facilitator for other businesses and industries that are looking to invest here, and have hosted dozens of organizations already. We plan to be a contributing force and an institution that lasts forever in Rwanda."[3]

A passion for helping Rwanda achieve its vision of economic growth has spread among other business leaders and entrepreneurs in the United States, Europe, and Australia. As President Kagame has told them in the words recalled by Dawson, "We have a huge vision for Rwanda. However, when we look around our country, we do not have enough talent to build the institutions and businesses we need. We need to borrow your talent and you need to teach us to do it for ourselves." Dawson notes that he's still working as an investment banker. "At Stephens I was helping corporate CEOs achieve their vision. I'm doing the same thing today, but my clients are a president and a bishop."

Today, Dawson serves on President Kagame's Presidential Advisory Council. The council draws top leaders from around the globe, including minister and bestselling author Rick Warren, Michael Porter from Harvard Business School, and former UK Prime Minister Tony Blair. The council meets every six months: in April in Kigali and September in New York to discuss projects that need to be undertaken (the latest initiatives focus on agriculture) and report their progress back to the president and the group.

Another endeavor Dawson is involved in is the Rwanda Presidential Scholars Program, which seeks to educate the top Rwandan students in math and science to become scientists, doctors, and engineers. With few facilities currently in Rwanda to educate them, the students are sent to schools in the United States at reduced tuition. By late 2009, a total of fourteen U.S. colleges participated in the education of over 150 students from Rwanda.

The next project is to build a university on the twenty-five-acre site of a former military base in Rwanda. The master plan calls for a facility that can board and educate 1,200 to 1,400 students with a curriculum that includes servant leadership, entrepreneurship, business, and engineering. A third project, spearheaded by Michael Fairbanks, co-founder of SEVEN Fund, a philanthropic foundation run by entrepreneurs, is to establish a Center for Entrepreneurial Excellence in Rwanda that will benefit all of Africa and explore private-sector solutions to poverty.

As Dawson spoke of the Rwanda projects, the passion was clearly back in his life. He has a deep and abiding purpose for the second half of his life, as well as a profound appreciation of what it means to be a leader. "When I was totally committed to my business career, it was way too limiting. Knowing President Paul Kagame and Bishop John Rucyahana and traveling to Africa have broadened my life. I see now that life turns pretty sour unless there are people who are willing to stand up and model integrity, passion, justice, and mercy. The entire world is dependent upon leadership."

No Regrets

Today, Dale Dawson enjoys a bigger purpose than he could have imagined in his days of being a "wheeler-dealer," and yet had it not been for those experiences he could not make the kind of contribution that will greatly benefit a country torn apart by genocide and in need of healing and hope. It is no wonder, then, that Dawson says he had no regrets in his life, although he does wonder at times what would have happened if at the age of twenty he had decided to engage in an "intensive faith walk." But if he had changed anything in his life, would he have garnered the necessary experiences that led him to what he is doing today? Perhaps not. "So, I don't second-guess it," Dawson concluded.

Dawson is a long way from the young boy growing up in Texas who rode in the milk delivery truck with his father, but the lessons learned at that young age continue to influence all that he does. In fact, Dawson credits his father with having a bigger influence on him than anyone else, and speaks with deep admiration for his mother, now in her eighties. Dawson readily shares the lessons he learned from his parents with others, particularly when he speaks to groups of students. His message encompasses family, "where you get your identity, your values, and your encouragement;" the importance of entrepreneurship and the belief "that there is always a way to make money;" and the secret to success: "if you work harder than everybody else you'll be fine."

Now, in the second half of his life, Dawson is aware of the impact that he and Judi are having on their two children, who are now college-aged. "They are really independent. I pray that they won't get hung up on someone else's definition of success," he observed. Just as his father influenced him, Dawson hopes to provide the same example to his children, especially not being afraid to change course in order to pursue what is most satisfying in life. "The truth is I don't know any other way to influence them more than the way I live. And I want them to be surrendered to whatever this divine hand pushes them to be; that they think about that and be conscious of it," he added.

This is also the essence of Dawson's advice to others who, like him, may have reached a point where passion has been extinguished and purpose is less clear. The problem may be one of perception: what you thought success meant was perhaps shaped by someone else's definition—and now that definition has lost its appeal or meaning. "Are you being led where you need to go? If not, don't be afraid to walk away," he said.

In life, everyone's story is unique, and each person's journey leads to a different destination. Yet as people follow their individual paths, there is comfort in knowing that someone else has faced many of the same questions and endured similar upheavals. Often it happens at midlife when people get stuck and wonder, what will I do next? Dawson's answer is to take the leap and find out. In the second half, it may be that the best is yet to come.

Notes

Chapter One

1. JetBlue.com, "An Apology from David Neeleman," accessed December 10, 2009, http://www.jetblue.com/about/ourcompany/apology/index.html

2. Adam Bryant, "Southwest Airlines to Buy Morris Air," *New York Times*, December 14, 1993, http://www.nytimes.com/1993/12/14/business/southwest-airlines-to-buy-morris-air.html

3. Stanford University, "High Tech, High Touch," April 30, 2003, http://ecorner.stanford.edu/authorMaterialInfo.html?mid=283

4. Stanford University, "High Tech, High Touch."

5. Bill George and Matthew D. Breitfelder, "David Neeleman: Flight Path of a Servant Leader," Harvard Business School Publishing, November 10, 2008.

6. George and Breitfelder.

7. JetBlue.com, "JetBlue Flies One Millionth Passenger and Announced More Than $100 Million in Flown Revenue for the Year," December 21, 2000, http://www.jetblue.com/about/pressroom/pressreleases/pr.asp?year=2000&news=12212000_millionpax

8. JetBlue.com, "JetBlue Announced Third Quarter Profit," November 7, 2001, http://www.jetblue.com/about/pressroom/pressreleases/pr.asp?year=2001&news=11072001_q32001

9. Sally B. Donnelly, "Blue Skies," *Time*, May 2, 2003, http://www.time.com/time/magazine/article/0,9171,168469-2,00.html

10. Greenleaf.org, Home Page, accessed December 10, 2009, http://www.greenleaf.org/whatissl/

11. Ian Mount, "David Neeleman, JetBlue," *Inc.*, April 1, 2004, http://www.inc.com/magazine/20040401/25neeleman.html

12. Jeff Benedict, *The Mormon Way of Doing Business: How Eight Western Boys Reached the Top of Corporate America* (New York: Warner Business Books), March 2008.

13. Jeff Bailey, "JetBlue's C.E.O. Is 'Mortified' After Fliers Are Stranded," *New York Times*, February 19, 2007, http://www.nytimes.com/2007/02/19/business/19jetblue.html

14. Bill George and Matthew D. Breitfelder.

15. YouTube.com, "David Neeleman Explains Feb. 14th," accessed December 10, 2009, http://www.youtube.com/watch?v=1V2ff3easYc&feature=related

16. JetBlue.com, "An Apology from David Neeleman."

17. JetBlue.com, "JetBlue Airways Names Dave Barger President and Chief Executive Officer; Founder David Neeleman Will Continue to Serve as Chairman of the Board," May 10, 2007, http://investor.jetblue.com/phoenix.zhtml?c=131045&p=irol-newsArticle&ID=998672&highlight

18. *The Economist*, "Missionary Man," August 27, 2009, http://www4.economist.com/node/14302634

19. Brendan Sobie, "Competition in Brazil Heats Up," August 20, 2009, http://www.flightglobal.com/articles/2009/08/20/331237/competition-in-brazil-heats-up.html

20. Jeffrey Sonnenfeld and Andrew Ward, *Firing Back: How Great Leaders Rebound After Career Disasters* (Boston: Harvard Business School Press), 2007.

Chapter Two

1. Stanford Graduate School of Business, "Charles Schwab & Co. Inc. (A): In 1999," February 22, 2000 (Revised September 18, 2003).

2. David S. Pottruck and Terry Pearce, *Clicks and Mortar: Passion Driven Growth in an Internet Driven World* (San Francisco: Jossey-Bass), 2001.

3. Stanford Graduate School of Business.

4. Lynda Applegate, F. Warren McFarlan, and Jamie Ladge, "Charles Schwab in 2002," Harvard Business School, Revised May 15, 2007.

5. Betsy Morris, "Charles Schwab's Big Challenge," *Fortune*, May 30, 2005, http://money.cnn.com/magazines/fortune/fortune_archive/2005/05/30/8261246/index.htm

6. Lynda Applegate, F. Warren McFarlan, and Jamie Ladge.

7. Betsy Morris.

8. Charles Schwab & Company, 2001 annual report.

9. Patrick McGeehan, "Charles Schwab to Give Up Title at Brokerage Firm," *New York Times*, February 1, 2003, http://www.nytimes.com/2003/02/01/business/charles-schwab-to-give-up-title-at-brokerage-firm.html?scp=7&sq=David%20Pottruck&st=cse

10. Riva D. Atlas, "Schwab Ousts Chief and Founder Steps In," *New York Times*, July 21, 2004, http://www.nytimes.com/2004/07/21/business/schwab-ousts-chief-and-founder-steps-in.html?scp=37&sq=David Pottruck&st=cse&pagewanted=

11. Zach Klitzman, "Talking Points—Pottruck: The Man Behind the Gym," *Daily Pennsylvanian*, October 29, 2008, http://thedp.com/node/57368

Chapter Three

1. Mara Der Hovanesian, "A New Rule Book for Fund Managers," *BusinessWeek*, September 4, 2000, http://www.businessweek.com/2000/00_36/b3697106.htm

2. CBSNews.com, "Paper Jam at HP," October 4, 2006, http://www.cbsnews.com/elements/2006/10/04/in_depth_business/timeline2063653.shtml

3. Patricia C. Dunn, "My Role in the Hewlett-Packard Leak Investigation," submission to the Subcommittee on Investigations, House Energy and Commerce Committee, September 28, 2006, http://republicans.energycommerce.house.gov/108/News/09282006_Testimony_Dunn.pdf

4. James Stewart, "The Kona Files: How an Obsession with Leaks Brought Scandal to Hewlett-Packard," *The New Yorker*, February 19, 2007, http://www.newyorker.com/reporting/2007/02/19/070219fa_fact_stewart?printable=true

5. CBSNews.com, "Patricia Dunn: I Am Innocent; Ousted Hewlett-Packard Chairwoman Talks to Lesley Stahl," October 8, 2006, http://www.cbsnews.com/stories/2006/10/05/60minutes/main2069430.shtml?source=RSSattr=60Minutes_2069430

6. Peter Burrows, "HP's Board Split over Dunn," September 11, 2006, *BusinessWeek*,http://www.businessweek.com/technology/content/sep2006/tc20060911_300418.htm

7. Robert Mullins, "Dunn Inducted into Hall of Fame," *PC World*, September 21, 2006, http://www.pcworld.com/article/127213/dunn_inducted_into_hall_of_fame.html

8. Patricia C. Dunn.

9. Stewart, "The Kona Files."

10. CBS11TV.com, "Judge Drops Charges Against Patricia Dunn," March 14, 2007, http://cbs11tv.com/technology/HP.Hewlett.Packard.2.500556.html

11. Patricia Sellers, "The Survival of Pattie Dunn," *Fortune*, May 31, 2007, http://money.cnn.com/magazines/fortune/fortune_archive/2007/06/11/100060831/index.htm

12. Patricia Sellers.

Chapter Four

1. Barnaby J. Feder, "Motorola Names Founder's Heir as Chief," *New York Times*, November 15, 1996, http://www.nytimes.com/1996/11/15/business/motorola-names-founder-s-heir-as-chief.html?scp=10&sq=Christopher%20Galvin%20and%20Motorola&st=cse

2. Paul Lucas and Maggie Overfelt, "Motorola Starting with His Earliest Foray into Car Radios, Paul Galvin Kept His Electronic Company Tuned in to New Waves of Technology with Remarkable Frequency," *Fortune,* April 1, 2003, http://money.cnn.com/magazines/fsb/fsb_archive/2003/04/01/341018/index.htm

3. Motorola Annual Report, 2002, Letter to Shareholders, http://www.motorola.com/General/Financial/Annual_Report/2002/letter04.html

4. Leslie Wayne, "Chief Decides to Step Down at Motorola," *New York Times,* September 30, 2003, http://www.nytimes.com/2003/09/20/business/chief-decides-to-step-down-at-motorola.html?scp=2&sq=Christopher-Galvin&st=cse

5. Barnaby Feder, "Motorola Picks an Outsider to Be a Chief Executive," *New York Times,* December 12, 2003, http://www.nytimes.com/2003/12/17/business/motorola-picks-an-outsider-to-be-its-chief-executive.html?scp=1&sq=Zander%20and%20turn%20up&st=cse

6. Greg Burns and Wailin Wong, "A Family Calling Has a New Direction," *Chicago Tribune,* April 13, 2008, http://www.harrisonst.com/images/stories/08–04–13_tribune_-_qa_with_chris_galvin.pdf

7. Laurie J. Flynn, "Ed Zander Steps Down as Chief Executive of Motorola," *New York Times,* November 30, 2007, http://www.nytimes.com/2007/11/30/business/worldbusiness/30iht-30moto.8548495.html?_r=1&scp=7&sq=Zander%20and%20Motorola&st=cse

Chapter Five

1. Keith Naughton, Kevin Peraino, Temma Ehrenfeld, Donna Foote, and Jamie Reno, "Who Killed Enron," *Newsweek,* January 21, 2002, http://www.newsweek.com/id/63622/page/1

2. *Harvard Gazette,* "Harper, Winokur to Join Harvard Corporation," February 10, 2002, http://www.news.harvard.edu/gazette/2000/02.10/corp.html

3. Bethany McLean and Peter Elkind, *The Smartest Guys in the Room: The Amazing Rise and Scandalous Fall of Enron* (New York: Portfolio, Updated Paperback Version), 2004.

4. Bethany McLean and Peter Elkind.

5. House Committee on Energy and Commerce, "Prepared Witness Testimony," Mr. Herbert S. Winokur, Jr., February 27, 2002, http://archives.energycommerce.house.gov/reparchives/107/hearings/02072002Hearing485/Winokur799print.htm

6. Kurt Eichenwald, "Enron's Many Strands: News Analysis; Talk of Crime Gets Big Push," *New York Times*, February 4, 2002, http://www.nytimes.com/2002/02/04/business/enron-s-many-strands-news-analysis-talk-of-crime-gets-big-push.html?scp=2&sq=Enron%27s+Many+Strands&st=nyt

7. Reed Abelson, "Enron Comes Under a Storm of Criticism," *New York Times*, December 16, 2001, http://www.nytimes.com/2001/12/16/business/business-enron-board-comes-under-a-storm-of-criticism.html?scp=2&sq=Enron+and+outside+directors&st=nyt

8. David H. Gellis and Catherine E. Schoichet, "Pug Winokur to Resign from Corporation," *The Harvard Crimson*, April 8, 2002, http://www.thecrimson.com/article.aspx?ref=180921

9. House Committee on Energy and Commerce, Prepared Witness Testimony.

10. House Committee on Energy and Commerce.

11. Herbert S. Winokur, "Some Common-Sense Advice for New Directors," *Directorship*, August 25, 2009, http://www.directorship.com/some-common-sense-advice-for-new-directors/

Chapter Six

1. Harry M. Jansen Kraemer Jr., "What Is this Thing Called CEO Leadership?" *Directors & Boards,* Fourth Quarter 2007.

2. Michael Arndt, "How Does Baxter's Harry Kraemer Do It?" *BusinessWeek*, July 22, 2002, http://www.businessweek.com/magazine/content/02_29/b3792088.htm

3. Michael Arndt.

4. Bill Bichard, "Citizen Kraemer: How Baxter International's Chief Harry Kraemer Learned to Stop Worrying and Love Sustainability," *Chief Executive*, February 1, 2002.

5. Keith H. Hammonds, "Harry Kraemer's Moment of Truth," *Fast Company*, October 2002, http://www.fastcompany.com/magazine/64/kraemer.html

6. Douglas Harbrecht, "Baxter's Harry Kraemer: 'I Don't Golf,'" *BusinessWeek*, March 28, 2002, http://www.businessweek.com/bwdaily/dnflash/mar2002/nf20020328_0720.htm

7. Keith Hammonds.

8. Baxter Annual Report 2002.

9. Baxter Annual Report 2003.

10. Michael Arndt.

11. "Company News; Baxter Says Chief Executive Will Resign," *New York Times*, January 27, 2004, http://query.nytimes.com/gst/fullpage.html?res=9406E4DF1538F934A15752C0A9629C8B63&scp=1&sq=Kraemer%20and%20Baxter%20and%20resign&st=cse

12. Baxter.com, "Baxter Announces Harry Kraemer to Resign as Chairman and CEO," January 26, 2004, http://www.baxter.com/about_baxter/news_room/news_releases/2004/01–26–04-kraemer.html

13. Susan Chandler, "Baxter's Ex-CEO Teaches Students: Do the Right Thing," January 7, 2007, http://archives.chicagotribune.com/2007/jan/07/business/chi-0701070112jan07

Chapter Seven

1. Richard Whiteley and Diane Hessan, *Customer Centered Growth: Five Proven Strategies for Building Competitive Advantage* (New York: Basic Books), 1997.

2. Ford.com, "Ford Focus Is Voted European Car of the Year 1999," November 17, 1998, http://media.ford.com/article_display.cfm?article_id=287

3. Robyn Meredith, "Ford Chairman to Stay on Past Usual Retirement Age," *New York Times*, March 14, 1997, http://www.nytimes.com/1997/03/14/business/ford-chairman-to-stay-on-past-usual-retirement-age.html?scp=44&sq=Nasser%20and%20Ford%20and%20CEO&st=cse

4. Danny Hakim, "Left in Nasser's Exhaust at Ford," *New York Times*, November 1, 2001, http://www.nytimes.com/2001/11/01/business/left-in-nasser-s-exhaust-at-ford.html

5. John Markoff, "A Web-Researched Ford in Microsoft's Future," *New York Times*, September 21, 1999, http://www.nytimes.com/1999/09/21/business/a-web-researched-ford-in-microsoft-s-future.html?scp=15&sq=Jacques%20Nasser&st=cse

6. Robyn Meredith, "G.M. and Ford in AOL and Yahoo Deals," *New York Times*, January 10, 2000, http://www.nytimes.com/2000/01/10/business/gm-and-ford-in-aol-and-yahoo-deals.html?scp=24&sq=Jacques%20Nasser&st=cse

7. PRNewswire.com, "Ford CEO Jac Nasser Announces Safety Initiatives During Congressional Testimony," September 6, 2000, http://www.prnewswire.com/cgi-bin/stories.pl?ACCT=104&STORY=/www/story/09-06-2000/0001306505&EDATE

8. PRNewswire.com, "Ford Board Reviews Firestone Tire Recall," September 14, 2000, http://www.prnewswire.com/cgi-bin/stories.pl?ACCT=104&STORY=/www/story/09-14-2000/0001313244&EDATE

9. David Barboza, "Bridgestone/Firestone to Close Tire Plant at Center of Huge Recall," *New York Times*, June 28, 2001, http://www.nytimes.com/2001/06/28/business/bridgestone-firestone-to-close-tire-plant-at-center-of-huge-recall.html?scp=3&sq=Firestone+tire+recall&st=nyt

10. *New York Times*, "Nasser Says Reductions in Jobs Won't Be Last Cutbacks at Ford," August 20, 2001, http://www.nytimes.com/2001/08/20/business/nasser-says-reductions-in-jobs-won-t-be-last-cutbacks-at-ford.html?scp=27&sq=Jacques%20Nasser&st=cse

11. Clive Mathieson and Matthew Stevens, "Jacques Nasser Replaces Don Argus at BHP Billiton," *The Australian*, August 4, 2009, http://www.theaustralian.news.com.au/story/0,24897,25882015-601,00.html

Chapter Eight

1. Zachary Schiller, "Value Pricing Pays Off," *BusinessWeek*, November 1, 1993, http://www.businessweek.com/archives/1993/b334329.arc.htm

2. Glenn Collins, "Procter & Gamble Chooses Its New Chief," *New York Times*, March 15, 1995, http://www.nytimes.com/1995/03/15/business/procter-gamble-chooses-its-new-chief.html?scp=1&sq=Edwin%20Artzt&st=cse

3. Mikolaj Jan Piskorski and Alessandro L. Spadini, "Procter & Gamble: Organization 2005 (A)," Harvard Business School, Revised October 4, 2007.

4. MarketingWeek.com, "Jager Hangs out P&G's Past to Dry," *Marketing Week*, September 17, 1998, http://www.marketingweek.co.uk/home/digest/2012007.article

5. MarketingWeek.com.

6. Richard Curtis, "New Swiffer Cleans Up for Procter," *Cincinnati Enquirer*, November 5, 1999, http://cincinnati.bizjournals.com/cincinnati/stories/1999/11/08/story2.html

7. Richard Curtis.

8. Mikolaj Jan Piskorski and Alessandro L. Spadini.

9. Chris Isidore and Martha Slud, "P&G Warning Hurts Dow," *CNN Money*, March 7, 2000, http://money.cnn.com/2000/03/07/companies/procter/

10. Mikolaj Jan Piskorski and Alessandro L. Spadini.

11. David Leonhardt, "Procter & Gamble Shake-Up Follows Poor Profit Outlook," *New York Times*, June 9, 2000, http://www.nytimes.com/2000/06/09/business/procter-gamble-shake-up-follows-poor-profit-outlook.html?scp=4&sq=Durk%20Jager%20CEO&st=cse

12. Geoffrey Colvin, "Boards to CEOs: One Strike and You're Out," *Fortune*, June 26, 2000, http://money.cnn.com/magazines/fortune/fortune_archive/2000/06/26/283008/index.htm

Chapter Nine

1. Leah Nathans Spiro, "Ticker Tape in the Genes," *BusinessWeek*, October 21, 1996, http://www.businessweek.com/1996/43/b3498157.htm

2. Kellogg School of Management, Northwestern University, Presentation by Jamie Dimon, October 4, 2002.

3. Patricia Crisafulli, *The House of Dimon: How JPMorgan's Jamie Dimon Rose to the Top of the Financial World* (John Wiley & Sons), 2009.

4. Kurt Eichenwald, "Business People; President of Primerica Surprised by Promotion," *New York Times*, September 26, 1991, http://www .nytimes.com/1991/09/26/business/business-people-president-of-primerica-surprised-by-promotion.html?scp=1&sq=Dimon%20and %20Primerica%20and%20Eichenwald&st=cse

5. Leah Nathans Spiro, "Smith Barney's Whiz Kid," *BusinessWeek*, October 21, 1996, http://www.businessweek.com/1996/43/b34981 53.htm

6. Leah Nathans Spiro.

7. Sharon R. King, "The Market Turmoil: Russia's Impact; Quick Action by U.S. Banks Limits Damage," *New York Times*, September 3, 1998, http://www.nytimes.com/1998/09/03/business/the-market-turmoil-russia-s-impact-quick-action-by-us-banks-limits-damage .html?scp=1&sq=Travelers%20Salomon%20and%20Russian% 20debt&st=cse

8. Peter Truell and Laura M. Holson, "Shaping a Colossus: The Industry; Gigantic Shadow over Wall Street," *New York Times*, April 7, 1998, http://www.nytimes.com/1998/04/07/business/shaping-a-colossus-the-industry-gigantic-shadow-over-wall-street.html?scp=15&sq= Citibank-Travelers%20merger&st=cse

9. Duff McDonald, *Last Man Standing: The Ascent of Jamie Dimon and JPMorgan Chase* (New York: Simon & Schuster), 2009.

10. Timothy L. O'Brien and Peter Truell, "Downfall of a Peacemaker; Heir Apparent's Departure May Signal Strain at Citigroup," *New York Times*, November 3, 1998, http://www.nytimes.com/1998/11/03/ business/downfall-peacemaker-heir-apparent-s-departure-may-signal-strain-citigroup.html?scp=2&sq=Dimon%20Fired%20Citigroup% 20president&st=cse

11. Ibid.

12. Patricia Crisafulli, *The House of Dimon*.

13. Kellogg School of Management, Northwestern University.

14. Daniel Kadlec, "Jamie Dimon: JPMorgan Chase," *Time*, December 17, 2004,   http://www.time.com/time/magazine/article/0,9171,1009783,00 .html#ixzz0Zxc7f0N0

15. Shawn Tully and Julie Schlosser, "The Deal Maker and the Dynamo," *Fortune*, February 9, 2004, http://money.cnn.com/magazines/fortune/ fortune_archive/2004/02/09/360092/index.htm

16. Patricia Crisafulli, *The House of Dimon*.

17. *Financial Times*, "Fifty Who Will Frame a Way Forward," March 10, 2009.

18. JPMorgan.com, "Jamie Dimon Speaks to HBS Graduates, Discusses Leadership Qualities," June 30, 2009, Http://www.jpmorgan.com/cm/ cs?pagename=JPM_redesign/JPM_Content_C/Generic_Detail_ Page_ Template&cid=1159391608440&c=JPM_Content_C

Chapter Ten

1. Autochannel.com, "AutoZone to Acquire TruckPro," March 2, 1998, http://www.theautochannel.com/articles/press/date/19980302/ press010365.html

2. Bob Buford, *Halftime: Moving from Success to Significance*, revised edition, (Grand Rapids, MI: Zondervan), 2009

3. OpportunityInternational.com, "World Relief, World Relief Canada, and HOPE International Partner with Opportunity International to Open Microfinance Bank for Rwanda's Poor," August 7, 2007, http:// www.opportunity.org/Page.aspx?pid=838

Acknowledgments

Without a doubt, a book is a team effort, and *Comebacks* is no different.

We thank our families for encouragement and commiseration, through all the ups and downs; for Andrea, her husband Bill Ferguson, her son David "Duke" Ferguson, her mother Ardis, and her brother Paul; for Tricia, her husband Joe Tulacz, her son Pat Commins, and Ben and Jeannie Zastawny and Bernadette and Stephanie Crisafulli.

A special thanks to Toni Ficaro for invaluable help arranging interviews, keeping schedules straight and us on track, and always being there; and to Katie Stack for ideas and support.

Thanks to many friends and other supporters too numerous to mention who helped immeasurably in the process, including Terri Savage, Ruth Fattori, Betsy Atkins, Keith VanderVeen, and Fari Hamzei.

At Jossey-Bass, our thanks to our editor, Genoveva Llosa, who championed the idea from the beginning and skillfully edited the book, and to the entire Jossey-Bass team, including Bernadette Blanco, Erin Moy, Cynthia Shannon, Gayle Mak, Mark Karmendy, and Suzanne Copenhagen.

To our agents, Doris S. Michaels and Delia Berrigan Fakis, at DSM Literary Agency, thank you for your enthusiasm, which helped bring this book into being.

Thanks to those who offered their wisdom and perspective in each of the profiles: Bob Buford, Diane Coutu, Judy Dimon, Leonard Elkun, Jim Hunter, Athena Katsaros, Paul Marshall, John McArthur, Bethany McLean, Terry Pearce, Jeffrey Sonnenfeld, and William White.

Our deepest gratitude goes to those who agreed to be interviewed for this book, candidly sharing their setbacks and comebacks. You are true leaders by your example: Dale Dawson, Jamie Dimon, Patricia Dunn, Christopher Galvin, Durk Jager, Harry Kraemer, Jacques Nasser, David Neeleman, David Pottruck, and Herbert Winokur.

About the Authors

Andrea Redmond is an independent consultant working with corporate boards, chief executive officers, and private investors on executive recruiting needs and succession and talent management activities.

Previously, Ms. Redmond spent twenty years with a highly regarded global executive search firm, as senior partner and co-head of the firm's CEO and board services practice. In addition to her leadership responsibilities, Ms. Redmond's activities included serving clients in the recruitment of directors for corporate boards and in identifying senior management across industries. She conducted numerous recruitment assignments for a variety of public companies and Fortune 500 firms.

Ms. Redmond earned a B.S. from Northern Illinois University and a master's in business administration from George Williams College. Ms. Redmond serves on the board of directors of Children's Memorial Hospital, Northwestern University Hospital, and the Robert H. Lurie Cancer Center. In January 2010, she joined the board of directors of The Allstate Corporation.

Patricia Crisafulli is an accomplished writer, author, and ghostwriter who has written numerous books. Ms. Crisafulli is the author of *The House of Dimon*, a leadership profile of JPMorgan Chase CEO Jamie Dimon, published by John Wiley & Sons in 2009 and featuring interviews with Dimon and other top Wall Street and business leaders.

A former business journalist, Ms. Crisafulli was a correspondent and deputy equities editor in the Chicago bureau of Reuters America. Her articles appeared in the *New York Times*, *Chicago Tribune*, *Boston Globe*, and other prestigious national newspapers. Her previously published works also include creative essays on Africa, Berlin, and Switzerland published in *The Christian Science Monitor*. In addition, she has written articles for the Leisure & Arts page of *The Wall Street Journal*.

She is also the author of a nonfiction book entitled *Remembering Mother, Finding Myself: A Journey of Love and Self-Acceptance*, published in 1999 by HCI Books Inc., (under the name Patricia Commins).

Index

233